A Sea of Faces
The Importance of Knowing Your Students

Donald H. Graves

HEINEMANN
Portsmouth, NH

Heinemann
A division of Reed Elsevier Inc.
361 Hanover Street
Portsmouth, NH 03801–3912
www.heinemann.com

Offices and agents throughout the world

Library of Congress Cataloging-in-Publication Data
Graves, Donald H.
   A sea of faces : the importance of knowing your students / Donald H. Graves.
      p. cm.
   Includes bibliographical references.
   ISBN-13: 978-0-325-00990-2
   ISBN-10: 0-325-00990-2
   1. Teacher–student relationships.   2. Teachers—Psychology.   I. Title.
   LB1033.G688 2006
   371.102'3—dc22   2006019537

Editor: Lois Bridges
Production: Patricia Adams
Typesetter: Gina Poirier Design
Cover design: Jenny Jensen Greenleaf
Manufacturing: Steve Bernier

Printed in the United States of America on acid-free paper
10   09   08   07   06   VP   1   2   3   4   5

To Betty Graves

Who Relishes the Company of Children

Contents

Acknowledgments

These poems actually began as prose pieces in Pat Werner's room on the Upper East Side of Manhattan. We were composing e-mails about the various children. Pat was always encouraging and had many questions for me about language. For example, I was concerned about using the word, "stoop." Was it an old word or one that survived the times? We decided to leave it in. Teachers need to know their children; Pat certainly knew all the various children in her room. She was a joy to work with.

I also read the poems aloud to my wife Betty, then Dr. Rob Richardson. I wanted Rob to listen to my descriptions of the children in poetic narrative to make sure they were consistently drawn.

A little more than a year ago I turned to poems over to Sue Ann Martin to read and share in her fifth-grade classroom. The children were very thorough with their comments. I am grateful to them for their hard work.

From time to time I have read these poems aloud to the Pine Tree School in New Hampshire, and in various local gatherings.

My editor, Lois Bridges, has been encouraging and put me in touch with others who could help with the manuscript.

Penny Kittle edited this manuscript, especially the poems. She claims she doesn't write poetry but she sure knows how to read the poems and point out all the little things an author needs to know. Penny laughed in all the appropriate places and fed me comments especially from the Pine Tree faculty. In one sense I feel as though this is "our" book—if she will allow me the privilege of including her.

My dear wife, Betty, has pushed and pushed to get this collection in print. She laughs and shares in the children's ills and delights. This book is dedicated to her.

Introduction

The purpose of this book is to help you get to know the children in your classroom. I have learned many approaches over fifty years of teaching that may be useful to you. Our children lead many lives in school and out. Facets of lives are revealed throughout the day, but about 75 percent of the stories that are on their tongues never get told.

Our days are pressured and we push children aside in order to get on with the lesson. The more I know a child, the more I can expect of him. When a student perceives my face as one with intelligent expectation, we have a challenging classroom. My face and my voice carry a tone that says, "You know things and I can't wait to find out what they are."

Chapter 1, "A Sea of Faces," shows how I strive to get to know my students by first memorizing the children's names. When I enter the classroom on day one, I know the names; it is just a matter of placing a name with a face. Calling a student by name is the beginning of respect for a child. While I am learning the names, I am also engaged in finding three nouns that will characterize each child. I may also choose three verbs that create pictures of what the child does. When children know that I want to get to know them alone and together, the community begins to grow.

Chapter 2, "Behold, the Class," introduces the notion that classes have personalities. Most of all I want the class to have things they do together. So much of teaching is geared for individuals. Children need to know where they are in a group. In this chapter, I introduce a ficticious fifth-grade class I worked with in Manhattan on the Upper East Side, taught by Ms. Burns (also a pseudonym for a teacher I created based on many years of observation and classroom experience). The dicta "Work hard; be kind; no excuses" encompasses so much of the activity in that classroom. When Ms. Burns encounters differences of opinion, she asks each child to speak the other's point of view. A class has to be conscious of choral speaking, music, construction, and drama in order to be a cohesive whole. Focusing on just individuals breeds a kind of selfishness too rampant in today's society.

All of the poems in Chapter 3, "One Classroom, Many Lives," take place in Ms. Burns' ficticious classroom in New York City. I have written at least ten poems about each of three boys: Marshall, Marco, and Amadeo. I have also written ten narrative poems about Gina, Stacy, and Rebekah. Finally, I have written ten poems about Ms. Burns. These children appear quite regularly in each other's narrative poems. I have attempted to cover their lives both in and out of school, as well as within the family. My sincere hope is that you will see your own children in these poems.

Narrative poems offer big thinking in a small space. You will see these children with all of their problems as well as their good points. We have to remember that we teach with high expectations. We approach children through their good points.

In Chapter 4, "Reflections for Discussion," I have written discussion points about each child for you and your staff to consider. Within each section are also discussion points for you to present to your students. Children are just as capable as teachers in discussing these narrative poems.

Chapter 5, "Listening," focuses on listening, the forgotten language art. I immediately show what listening entails and then expand that listening to an entire building in San Diego, California.

1

A Sea of Faces

September 2006 marks my fiftieth anniversary teaching school. I began teaching seventh-grade reading and science. I taught with only eight weeks of teacher preparation from an intensive summer program. The shortage of teachers was so great that the state of Massachusetts offered courses to assist the public schools.

Helen Porter, principal of the East Fairhaven School, who observed me teaching in the summer, said, "This will be the last time you'll ever see twelve children in your class." I was oblivious to her meaning. "In fact," she said, "you'll be teaching thirty-nine seventh graders." If she thought I could handle the situation, I would, no big deal.

On that first day the children kept filing in while casting furtive glances at me, studying me, wondering who I was, and pondering their next moves. I wasn't used to having so much scrutiny. One boy, David Brown, stared at me with large brown eyes. I stared back. "What does your staring mean?" I challenged. He challenged.

I lost my plan about ten that morning and had to teach the rest of the day by telling stories and reading aloud. A sea of faces tilted upward. They paid attention for a while but soon grew restless. The students began to talk, nudge, and poke at each other. I was teaching on the fly; they knew it and I knew it. I was totally exhausted at the end of the day and sat in a stupor, wondering what I'd ever do the next day.

I wanted the class to like me. What I didn't realize is that students don't like you unless you know the details that allow you to like them. Further, I needed to know the details of how they learned, what they wanted, and what interested them. Such detail was beyond me, so I taught them as a whole group.

Tone is important. I wonder what the principal or other teachers would have thought had they listened from the corridor. I was just out of the U.S. Coast Guard. I imagined I was the students' commanding officer barking out orders. I had to be in control, be the authority on all subjects, and grant permission to go to the bathroom or to take another piece of paper. The tone of authority begins in the belly, moves through the chest, and pours from deep in the throat. Occasionally, we need to use that tone, but not *all the time*, as in my early teaching days.

When I walk the corridors in a school, I listen for a variety of tone. Voice controls tone. Malcolm Gladwell, in his book *Blink* (2004), describes this as he listens to partners speaking in a marriage, as the chair addresses the board, or as a doctor speaks to a patient. Their tones suggest complete authority, sometimes modulated, and in rare cases, the silence of listening and attending.

Once in a while I'd pick up a shard of information while the students were busily filling in my profile. Of course, the children are filling in the details of our personalities. They talk about me at recess. "Is he strict? Does he yell? Do you think he likes us? How can we get him mad?"

Two days into teaching, my wife, Betty, had our second child, Alyce. The good news is that she arrived on a Saturday so I could recover by Monday. But my preparation for Monday's class was less than adequate.

Five days into teaching, my wife and I bought a used 1953 Dodge coupe. I drove into the school lot in our new car. Within five minutes I was confronted in class by three boys.

"See you got a new car."

"Fifty-three Dodge Hydramatic."

"Is that the best you could do?"

As Penny Kittle writes in Public Teaching (2003, 15), "We are their entertainment." The children mimic us, laugh at us, and choose details for their own little playlets.

It is a long way from seeing a sea of faces to seeing individuals. And it is a long way from seeing individuals to knowing what is significant in their lives. I've been pondering shortcuts for nearly fifty years. Although you may not be able to apply the shortcuts, you will at least be able to understand what territories are involved.

Three-Column Exercise

My first move is to memorize the names of the children. I circle the number of students and post it in the upper right-hand corner of my paper. Sometimes I have three to four classes to learn student names. This takes time but learning about students begins with their names. I am curious about ethnic backgrounds. Sometimes I ask a student, "Tell me the story of your name." Some students don't like their name because they were named after a parent, aunt, uncle, or grandmother they don't respect or because the name is from another era.

Some of them cringe as they go out to the playground. I moved to East Greenwich, Rhode Island, when I was in fourth grade. I was immediately given a nickname, Rabbit, because I was small and especially because I had big ears. I didn't like the name and had to endure its use until I moved away to New Jersey three years later. Of course, as I got to know my friends in Rhode Island I got used to the name; they just spoke it automatically.

After I have memorized the names in alphabetical order, I begin to stick some traits next to each name. I memorize the names from beginning to end, or I try to write them from memory. Of course, I first learn the bright and the tough students; they are memorable. It is the children who are less engaged that are difficult.

I try to place solid nouns opposite each name. William Carlos Williams writes, "No ideas but in things." For the column opposite Timmy, I write: football, books, desk. And for Alison I write: sweater, pen, braces, sewing, recess, CDs. It is up to me to fill in the details that characterize each student. See Figures 1–1 and 1–2 for my two trials in learning the students' names. Figure 1–1 shows my first memory attempt for one class, on the second day of school.

Beyond the learning of names, in some way I need to confirm that the child knows what I have observed. Remember, the children in the middle, the ones who want to be part of the woodwork, are the ones to whom you must especially pay attention. I can put an X in the third column if I can confirm with specifics: "I see you made quite a catch at second base. I didn't know you could run so fast," or "What's the story behind you hating green beans?"

Figure 1–2 shows my final attempt at learning the children's names, a week after school had begun. Note that the third column is filling in.

This book is about absorbing the lives of your children. Until they know you are in the process of absorption, their will to learn may be suspect. I can't make children learn, but at least I can provide solid appointments for learning.

Nancie Atwell tells the story of B. J. Sherman. She says, "Until I could put writing in the path of what he wanted to say I was wasting my time with him. In this case B. J. wanted to write about going to live with his father. He tried personal narrative and it didn't work. I suggested that he switch to fiction and that freed him up to express" (phone conversation).

What do I learn from this incident? The first thing is that Nancie was searching for a way to help B. J. Indeed, she was actively searching for each one of her students. The second is that she saw that writing was a means to B. J.'s own ends. The third is that she had a hunch that fiction, the chance to be free from the accuracy of events, would allow him to tell his story. This is

First Memory Attempt

	Experiences and Interests	Confirmation Column
1. Fred Gallo	Sharks	
2. Marcella Cowan	Horses	X
3. John Pringle		
4. Allison Goodrich		
5. Norman Frazier	Sister in hospital	X
6. Delores Sunderland	Sea life, birds	
7. Frances Sawtelle		
8. Johnathan Freedman	Prehistoric animals	
9. Charles Lentini	Motorcycles	
10. Aleka Alphanosopoulos	Singing	
11. Jason Beckwith		
12. John Finlayson		
		**
13. Joel Cupperman		
14. Mark Andrade		
15. Patricia Rezendes		
16. Betty Oliver		
17. Margaret Texeira		
18. Marcus Washington		
19. Patricia Show		
20. William Frost		
21. Paul Gardner		
22. Jason Tompkins		
23. Ford Park		
24. Laurie Kunstler		
25. Albert Guimond		

** All children below the line were not remembered on first attempt on the second day of school

Figure 1–1. First memory attempt

the art of teaching: to observe, to pick up the details of our students and piece them together for successful teaching, and to know the process so well that options become obvious.

I am in the process of learning about how to use my iPod, a nice device for playing music wherever I am. But I became so tangled with directions and wires that I had to hire Sean Doucette to make sense of the situation. (Yes,

Second Memory Attempt

	Experiences and Interests	Confirmation Column
1. Marcella Cowan	Horses, birth of foal	X
2. Norman Frazier	Sister well, fishing	X
3. Jonathan Freedman	Tyrannasaurus rex, brontosaurus, draws well	X
4. Marcus Washington	Athlete, kick ball	
5. Delores Sunderland	Any craft, especially painting, sea life	X
6. Jon Finlayson	Football, collects cards of athletes	X
7. Betty Oliver	Takes care of little sister, cooks	X
8. John Pringle		
9. Frances Sawtelle	Cat and kittens	
10. Ford Park	Works with father on road-moving equipment on Saturdays	X
11. Joel Cupperman		
12. Jason Beckwith		
13. Fred Gallo	Sharks, movie "Jaws"	
14. Aleka Alphanosopoulos	Collects records	X
15. Charles Lentini	Collects motorcycle brochures, brother has cycle	
16. Allison Goodrich		
17. Mark Andrade	Fishes with father	
18. Jason Tompkins		
19. Paul Gardner		
20. Margaret Texeira	Cares for little brother and sister, this angers her	X
		**
21. Albert Guimond		
22. Patricia Snow		
23. Patricia Rezendes	Knows something about weaving	
24. William Frost		
25. Laurie Kunstler		

** All children below the line were not remembered on second attempt one week after school started.

Figure 1–2. Second memory attempt

the simple iPod.) I watched his face as he used cold logic, yes or no, to get to the bottom of my problems. I wanted the iPod to connect in with my main sound system. His face showed calm and confidence. What struck me was that he kept trying one solution after another until he hit the right one. This was a puzzle he had to solve.

Of course, Sean was dealing with inanimate problems. Human ones are quite different. On the other hand, our calm demeanor in the face of the learner's upset can go a long way toward a solution. I may ask the child, "I'm sure you've thought about this a great deal; what might you try next? Relax a minute and give me a hint." If the learner can't think of something, I'll say, "Experiment with this."

Sadly, when learners don't want to work or can't solve problems, we blame ourselves. Sometimes we blame the student.

Invitation

Choose one of your children and do a quick write for about five to six minutes. Write it in the first person and the present tense. I wrote through Timmy's eyes:

> I am the smallest kid in my classroom. I have to keep my eye on two kids who beat on me. Jason and Ricky say, "Hi Twerp," and then they belt me on the arm. I go way over to the edge of the playground and play with Andy who is about my size. But they find me. I wish I could just swing and hit one of them in the stomach but then it is two against one.

And next I took my quick write and turned it into a poem.

Why Poetry?

I choose poetry because it can be written quickly and concisely. Nancie Atwell says, "Writing begins with poetry. Everything about writing can be taught through poetry" (phone conversation). Poetry is big thinking in a small space. I may start with prose, but my second revisions go right into poetry.

> I am the smallest,
> The shortest,
> The pigmy,
> The runt,
> The rabbit.

Jason and Ricky
Beat on me.
They bunch their fists,
Crack me on my arm,
Trip me, push me.

Just once, oh just once
I'd like to spin,
And plant my fist
In Ricky's gut.

Do I dare?
Can I?
Will I?

Now I will write through Cindy's eyes:

I love to go to the cafeteria. I like to eat but mostly I like to sit with my friends: Kathy, Willie, and Jean. We comment on the food but mostly we talk about the other kids like Rosalie. Every day Rosalie sits alone. She's just different so we study her clothes and what she eats. Her clothes aren't much.

And here is the poem.

About 11:50 I follow
Kathy, Willie, Jean
To the cafeteria.
I follow them,
Not the smell of pizza.

We sit together
On a bench,
Lean into our conversation
Across the table
So we can talk
        About girls, boys,
            Who are cute, who are not.
There is Rosalie
And her oily, stinking sandwich,

Her dress with the patch
On it. I tell Willie
She is so ugly
It makes me want
To puke.

Now I will write through Rosalie's eyes:

I wish Mom would make American sandwiches like ham and cheese on
white bread. The oil from my sandwich drains all over the table top. I can't
resist looking up to see if anyone notices. Cindy notices, puts her hand
across her mouth while smiling and talks to Kathy and Willie. I wonder
what they are saying about me.

Here is the poem from the prose.

This wreck of a sandwich,
This oily, soaking bread.
With tomatoes and olives
Leaking on to the table.

I wish Mom would make
American sandwiches
With cheese and ham
On white bread.

The oil is on my fingers,
Draining down my arm.
I cast a glance at Cindy
Who is watching.

She says something
Behind her hand
To Willie, Kathy, and Jean
And I know,
I mean I know
It is about me.

About five years ago, I was interviewing a woman about her junior high
school days. She was plenty upset when the oil drained from her Italian sand-

wich. The small picture is draining oil. The big picture is she wants to be American. That is her wish. I used my knowledge of that woman to consider what it might be like for a child in my class to wish to be American.

Quick writes give you a fast sketch of a child. As you did this, you may have been conscious of the process of placing nouns and verbs in the text. If not, change some of the nouns and verbs after you've written. Writing or attempting a poem means taking those nouns and exploding the moments in the words. Keep asking, What does this child want? and then write from the child's point of view. Try to write three poems through the eyes of the child that you did a quick write for.

What Does Writing Do?

Writing is different than speaking. I could tell someone about what it was like to be small and in the fourth grade. But when I simply write, "I am the smallest kid in fourth grade," I immediately say, "So what does that mean?" and I stop and ponder it. That's the difference between speech and writing. In writing I can look back over the line and think. Thought gets slowed down and I wonder about the big and small pictures here. How do kids react to me?

I stop, ponder, and write. I also write with very low standards. That is the way it is with first-draft writing. I know that I will return to rewrite this text.

Consider this review of writing poetry. Here is my section on moving from prose to poetry. It is characterized by

1. *Repetition*—Certain lines or words are repeated.
2. *Exaggeration*—I pack in the emotion. Events are larger than life itself.
3. *Narrative*—The story unfolds.
4. *Strong nouns and verbs at the end of the lines*—I rarely use prepositions.
5. *First person* and *present tense*—The poem is written through the child's eyes. I become the child as I write.

What Are the Children's Wishes?

Wishes or wants shape narratives. Something stands in the way and I write that in.

In the first instance, Timmy doesn't like to be picked on. He wishes he could fight.

Cindy wants to maintain her group of friends but at another's expense.

Rosalie wishes her mother wouldn't make Italian sandwiches. But she also wishes she could be part of some group. She wonders how to be accepted.

Narratives are built around the wishes of the main characters. Children quite naturally have wishes, both for the small picture and the big picture.

Sharing About Yourself

One of the prime rules in journalism is "Share information in order to get information." Children are like vacuum cleaners; they suck up any bits of information about us they can. But why not do it overtly through your own writing? Children are perceptive. Unless you are invested in your piece, they won't be invested in their own. This is also a new venture for many. A good share of the children, especially the older ones, will not involve themselves emotionally. Voice, so closely related to emotion, is what drives the writing ahead. It is also critical that I share a wide range of emotion in order to bring children into the process. When I speak of a wide range of emotion, I mean the following: shame, regret, joy, humor, embarrassment, sadness, excitement, anger. That's the short list.

Remember, emotion is the engine of the intellect. Unless I can show emotion through my narratives, it will be difficult for students to show a range of emotion in their own texts. Notice that I rarely use adjectives and adverbs: *angry, sad, joyful, miserable.* The real job is to show the emotion by what the character does.

Young women are very different than young men in this regard. They easily slip into a character, and their characters reflect. Men are different. They project emotion in what their main character does. "I put a move on the goalie and slapped the puck beyond his reach." I might ask the author, "Tell me about all of the feelings associated with scoring."

Here is a poem I wrote through the eyes of Rebekah. You will meet Rebekah later on, in Chapter 3. Rebekah is ten and is a very sensitive child. She lives in New York and ponders the meaning of the bombings on September 11, 2001.

One Day
One day, three years ago,
When the fire engines
Were screaming in the streets

And smoke was in the air,
I heard about the terrorists
Who drove planes
Into the Twin Towers.

I asked Mama
Who did that,
And she said there are people
Who hate us,
Who hate our country.

I asked her
Do they hate me?
No, they don't hate you,
They just hate us
All together.

We talked about it
At school; it was on the radio,
On TV, and I still wonder
What we did
To make them so angry,
That they'd give their lives
Just to punish us.

When I go to bed
I wonder what
I have done wrong
To bring so much hate.

Final Reflection

When you first viewed your children, they were a sea of faces. Some stood out;
a few were very loud, many were quiet. The beginning of knowing a child
starts with the child's name. Even before my first class I want to learn their
names in alphabetical order. In some classes children are coming and going,
meaning that the list doesn't get stabilized until the second week.

I go through two memory attempts. Above all I want children to be repre-
sented with at least three strong nouns, followed by three strong verbs. Of

course, as the year continues the nouns and verbs will change. Remember the Williams quote, "No ideas but in things."

I invited you to become a child and write prose for five minutes through the child's eyes. You probably chose a child who stood out and displayed good nouns and verbs. Finally, I asked you to write three poems based on the narrative you sketched about the child. These may have been the first poems you've ever written. No matter; you lowered your standards and got words down on the page.

This book is about absorbing the lives of your children. You have worked hard to get started on this important journey.

2

Behold, the Class

I listened in on two teachers discussing their children in September.

Angie: So, Tina, how's your class this year?
Tina: Well, Angie, I think they are quite restless, talkative; they don't understand my directions.
Angie: Don't forget the class you left behind in June. You had everything down pat with them.
Tina: I know. I know. It just seems that I'm working awfully hard, maybe harder than I did last fall. Teaching is tough work . . . and then there are the tests.
Angie: Don't remind me of the tests.

You have been working hard to get to know your children as individuals. On the other hand, classrooms have personalities of their own. Some are loud, talkative; some are soft and tough to get responses from. Only a few are near ideal.

This chapter is about building a classroom and establishing a community of learners, much as Ms. Burns has done in Chapter 3. Ms. Burns is firm, challenging, but constantly building relationships between children. See the relationship between Amadeo and Marshall regarding the sickness of Marshall's dog (see the poems about Marshall, Amadeo, and Mrs. Burns in Chapter 3). Witness her challenge to the team studying immigration (see the poems about Gina and Amadeo in Chapter 3).

On the other hand, neither the class nor Ms. Burns ever knows when Marshall will explode. Reading brings tears to his eyes. Ms. Burns can't predict when a soft remark will bring an incendiary response. His cauldron is constantly boiling. When it will boil over is anyone's guess.

Witness Rebekah's listening to Marshall (see "Poor Marshall" on page 90). The teacher cannot be everywhere with every child's upset; for this reason the teacher must provide standard negotiating procedures. Not all children can negotiate, but if eight can be successful negotiators the class will become a strong community.

Fostering Strong Negotiators

Building strong negotiators is a never-ending process. It may take a full year before some of the children can build a repertoire for negotiating. Some cases are simple, some difficult. Taking another child's point of view, especially when a direct threat is implied, is especially taxing.

Child A: Why did you take my pencil?
Child B: You've got other pencils in your desk.
Child A: The least you could have done is to ask permission.
Child B: Well, I'm just borrowing it.
Child A: Fine, then give it back right now.
Child B: Just let me finish this last paragraph.
Child A: No, I want it now.

There isn't much in the way of emotional recognition in this interchange. One person took the pencil without consideration for the feelings of the other. Neither does the second party consider the need for the other to "just finish the paragraph." The system that works across all subjects (yes, all subjects) is to ask each party for her account of the event. Secondly, listen for any emotional content from either party. Thirdly, recognize the emotional content. Fourthly, ask the parties what their hope is for the outcome of the conflict. Start with the outcome. In some situations and depending on the tension in the situation, negotiations begin with the fourth step.

Notice how Ms. Burns helps Stacy deal with not wanting to be Puerto Rican (see "Solutions" on page 63). Any problem connected to ethnicity will take more than one session. She recognizes the emotional content of Stacy's upset yet will not compromise on Stacy's need to investigate other sources for help.

Using the Language

In some situations you have to act quickly for the safety of the class. When Marshall explodes, or threatens other children, it is important to act and act decisively. If Marshall is at his wit's end and blurts, "Make me!" Ms. Burns will walk directly to Marshall, look him in the eye, and say in a soft voice:

You have probably been thinking about this a long time. Tell me about your thinking. You may not be able to answer right now, but I'll be back in fifteen minutes.

Her implication is that Marshall has been thoughtfully building up to this moment. Of course, he may not have been thinking about this at all, and her question allows him to ponder the issue. Reactive children, especially Marshall, need time to think.

Other children are observing this showdown between Marshall and the teacher. She moves directly to where he has spoken, looks him in the eye, and states in a small voice, "You can't answer right now, but I'll be back." In short, the children are learning how to deal with an explosive situation.

Ms. Burns isn't the perfect teacher. Here is a poem illustrating a bad day:

Ms. Burns Loses It
The day began
with a certain restless sound.
Children argued, chairs scraped.
After recess the noise increased.
"Get out of my way,"
Marshall shouts
With his hands
on Marco's shoulders.
"Ms. Burns, Marco just shoved
Me against the wall."
"Marshall, stop it."
"Why do you always call
my name?"

"I'm not in the mood
for an argument.
You and Marco
over here, now!"
Ms. Burns eyes crackled fire;
Her voice rose, "Be still
This minute. This is no time
For a discussion."
She hissed as she spoke.
The room is still.
Mouths drop to see Ms. Burns
Shout and hiss.

Later, she calls
The class together
And says, "What did you notice
With Marshall and Marco?"

No one spoke.
Just the sound of the hamster
Racing in his cage.
Rebekah said, "I think
You lost it, Ms. Burns."
Ms. Burns waited,
And slowly looked
Into the face
Of each of the children
And said, "I apologize."

Teachers have power. Your power is greatest at the point of a well-timed apology. Ms. Burns has been carefully building a social fabric that will allow children to function independently. But she is a big part of the social fabric. Most of us have days that occasionally make us cross and we bark at the children. We enjoy our power and the quiet of the classroom after we bark or command. On the other hand if the frequency of our bark is too great, then an apology is in order. After all, if the children need to apologize to each other, we need to as well.

Getting Lost in the Group

We focus on individuals and teams of individuals who are learning to negotiate. Sometimes we ask for a desired outcome when addressing a group. We focus on the end product of behaviors. "OK, how is your team going to solve this? Give me different outcomes. You have some choices to make. I'll be back in fifteen minutes and I want you to have your choice made. Remember, sometimes you have to live with difficult options. You have to give up something for the good of the group."

Now it is time to move to larger venues that involve the entire class. There will be less negotiation. Choral speaking, singing, or movement and dance give rise to the joy of expression. During times of transition, all of these all-class approaches have application. How well I remember standing on the playground at Central Elementary in San Diego and listening to children sing as they marched to recess or lunch.

Think over your day or times of transition. What is it that you do as an entire group? Think over the *we*; think over what the class has accomplished together as an entire group.

Consider projects that are in service of others. Walk through your neighborhood. Send half of the class in one direction, the other half the opposite way. Take photos with digital cameras with both groups. Interview people you encounter.

Carmen Fuertes, a ten-year-old child, (*L. A.* January 1995 pp. 12–18) teaches how her class explores her block:

> We split up. One half starts on this side of the block and goes in the opposite direction of the other half of the class. That's to make sure we don't miss anything. when we get back we compare what each group saw. I remember yesterday when we walked, and we met like halfway around. We said to the other guys, "You'll never see what we saw. You'll be too late. Hah hah ha!" What we saw was a accident right when it happened. Two cars scratched fenders, and one guy was real mad because he had a new car. We started taking pictures right away.
>
> See, when we go for a walk on our block, we get down everything. We already have a computer picture of what our block looks like on all four sides. We use our video camera to do a layout of everything. Then when things happen, we can put a button on the screen with a date on it; so, if you call for the button, it will give you more detail. For example, if you want to see yesterday's accident, call for the button. Then you can see people standing around the accident, the policeman, and the two men. We couldn't interview the men, but we did talk to the policeman. He couldn't comment on that accident, but we did ask him about accidents in the area 'cause this is his beat. Tomorrow, three kids from our classroom will go to the police station to find out about auto accidents around our block. We haven't done this before.

Choral Speaking

Consider choral speaking as an approach to developing an all-class spirit. In the space of one week I can teach a class at least three poems that they can recite any time of day and in any location.

You will find many poems for choral speaking on pages 144 and 145 in *Explore Poetry* (Graves 1990).

We often lose that sense of collaborative power, the power of individuals who have a place in a group that is going somewhere and has a sense of self, "We can do these things." You can probably recall moments in your own education when you participated in a play, sang in a chorus or musical, or played on a team. There was joy in sensing the power of the group. Choral speaking enables us to have a sense of ourselves several times a day. Naturally, learning the possibilities of language, tasting the sound and rhythm, and getting to know more poets are valuable carry-overs as well.

Final Reflection

We can know all about individual children in our classroom, but a group of individuals devoid of any sense of community is not going anywhere. I can know all about Marshall as a dog lover, all about him as a ballplayer, and all about his dislike of reading, but until he becomes a community member, the class is not going anywhere and neither is Marshall.

3

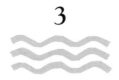

One Classroom, Many Lives

*T*his chapter spotlights Ms. Burns and several of her students. There are ten or more poems written about each child and ten about Ms. Burns. There are two routes you can take. The first is to listen to the poems on the website (*www.heinemann.com*) to get a sense of each child as well as how a teacher (such as Ms. Burns) would address them individually and as a group. The second is to read the poems. You might find it informative to list the nouns that are important to each child. In addition, each child lives, moves, and accomplishes. Make a list of those verbs.

When you have finished reading or listening to the poems, you may enjoy discussing some of the issues in the lives of these children. There are discussion ideas for teachers as well as for children and teachers to review together. Enjoy the journey.

Disclosure

For five months I followed children in a particular classroom in New York City. I first wrote narratives about the children, but the narratives were composite accounts of certain events that went on in the classroom. Further, the children in this room bear no resemblance to any child living or deceased. On the other hand, the wishes and desires of these children are readily found in any child. I shifted the narrative prose accounts to poetry, through which I could get to the heart of each child's wishes more quickly.

Marshall

Marshall

I am the biggest kid in fifth grade;
Nobody messes with me.
I can take any kid in our class,
And I can even take every kid
In sixth grade, except for three.
Maybe by June I can take them too.

I live with my Granny.
She says, "Somebody's got to do it."
Granny has white hair
And a nice smile,
But she can be mean
Like making me stay
On the stoop when I forget
To feed our dog, Sullivan.

The kids on my block
Speak with squawky voices.
They say, "Let's go to the park
And play baseball, Marshall.
Granny won't know."
They know if I leave that stoop
All hell will break on me.
I say, "Leave me alone
Or I'll beat you up.
Get outta here."
When they run they
Say teasing things
Back at me.

Granny's Dog, Sullivan

Sullivan is a humungous dog
With mopey eyes
That peek at you funny.
Granny says I have to walk
Him morning and night,
Feed him in the afternoon
And pick up his poop
From the street and put
It in a little bag. Disgusting!
She says I got to learn
Responsibility. Disgusting!

I ask her where he got
Such a dumb name.
She says Sullivan
Was her favorite uncle.
I don't get it.

But every morning
When I reach for his leash
He starts to dance.
His nails make clickety-clack
Sounds on the linoleum.

When Sullivan poops
He looks embarrassed.
I look around to see
Who is looking.
I feel silly when
Someone is looking.
So I don't pick up his poop.

When I look at TV
Sullivan puts his chin
On my knee,
I pat the couch
And say, "Wanna come up?"
He springs up,

Nestles next to me.
When I look down at him
He reaches his head up
And licks me on the nose.

Sick Sullivan

Sullivan isn't eating,
Lies in the corner
Looks at me with his big eyes,
And doesn't lift his chin.
I shake the leash
and he won't
Even get up. Granny
Says he hasn't moved all day.

Next day when I get up
I look for him. I'm worried
That Sullivan might die;
We just don't know
What's the matter with him.

Granny opens her purse
And shows me she
Doesn't have the money.
But tomorrow
We're off to the Vet's.
Sullivan is so big
We can't pick him up.
Granny asks Mr. Caruso
Who has a dog so he knows
What to do. Get a blanket,
I'll take two corners, he says
you get one each.

Down the street we go,
Catch the Lexington Avenue,
Up to Dr. Cowan's,
All kinds of animals there,
Some barking, some sick,
Some cats in little cages,
A girl holding a rabbit,
A crazy, noisy place.

Dr. Cowan is a woman
With kind eyes and gentle hands,
She smiles and talks dog talk,
A little voice, quiet sounds.
We ask, what's the matter?
Tell us please.
She looks him all over,
Checks his blood, listens
And listens. Finally she says,
I just don't know.
It may be his heart.
We've got to keep him
Here for observation.

I shout, "You can't keep him,
He sleeps on my bed. I need
To take him for walks."
She shakes her head and smiles,
"No Marshall, he can't walk;
He's too weak.
Let us help you.
Call us tomorrow;
We'll let you know."

Working It Out

I miss Sullivan,
Only dog I ever had,
And I need him;
I'd like to punch someone
To make them hurt like I do.
I know it would feel good.

Granny says I got an attitude,
And I do. So what?
I yell at her to leave me alone.
On the way to school
I kick a garbage can
And it makes a loud noise.
At school I look for a fight.
Someone like Amadeo.
A punky kid, a twerp.
I give him a shove,
And then trip him,
He tries to slink away.
Ms. Burns says, "I saw that.
You two over here."

She doesn't yell,
Says I heard about your dog
From your Granny.
I could feel the tears come.

But that twerp Amadeo says,
"I had a dog once,
The one I drew
Up on the bulletin board.
His name was Lightning
But a car killed him in the street."

I ask, "What kind was he?"
"Just a mutt, got him at the pound,
But mutts are smart."
I say, "My dog is smart too
But now he's at the Vet's
And they don't know
What's wrong."
I could feel the tears again,
And I feel stupid to cry.
I look at Ms. Burns;
She has a kind look on her face.

"Amadeo, how come you didn't
Get another dog?"

"Cuz we moved
And we can't have a dog.
In our new apartment."

"You could come see my dog,
When the Vet finds out what's wrong."

Coming Home

We picked Sullivan
Up on Saturday.
When the Doc let
Him out of his pen.
I was so happy.
I got down and hugged him;
He licked my face
Like I was his best friend
We walked all the way home.
He's my dog alright.
He kept looking up at me
To see if I was still there.

The doctor said Sullivan
Needs a new diet.
She said his heart wasn't good.
She tried a new medicine
And his heart is better
Granny said the doctor
Give it to us for free.

Amadeo Pays a Visit

I ask Amadeo for his phone number.
He looks at me funny
Like he doesn't trust me;
He needs to see Sullivan.
My Granny will call his Mom
But he says his Mom works weird hours.
We'll keep trying.
Maybe he'll come,
Maybe he won't.

Saturday morning our buzzer
Goes off; Sullivan barks,
Amadeo is downstairs
With his Mom. His Mom knocks
But I don't see Amadeo
Cuz he's behind her.
The women talk
And I say, "Here's Sullivan;
He's bigger than you are."
Amadeo looks scared.

"What I mean is,
He's just a big dog."
Amadeo pats Sullivan on the head,
Kneels down, puts his hand out,
And says, "Give me your paw."
Sullivan just looks at him.
"Don't he know how to do that?"
"No, he don't."
"We can teach him then."
Pretty soon Sullivan sits,
Gives his paw.

I've got one smart dog.

Meet the Coach

Granny turns off the TV.
"You waste too much time
Sitting on the couch.
Come with me."
She takes me and Sullivan
To the park to meet the coach.

"Can you teach him
To play baseball?"
"How old are you?" says Coach.
"Ten."
"Hmm, big kid for ten.
Throw me this baseball."
He goes back about thirty feet
And I burn one in.
He has a little smile
Like he don't believe it.
He goes back fifty feet.
This time I put my whole
Body into it, and his smile
Gets bigger. "Okay, you show
Up for practice
Right after school tomorrow."
He talks to Granny,
And his eyes get real wide.

Granny Tells a Story

I wanna tell you a story,
A true story about your Grampa,
God rest his soul.
You throw a baseball
Just like him. You both
Have it natural,
Like you was born with it.

Nobody could hit
Grampa's flame thrower,
Know what I mean?
He had those hitters
Guessing what would come
Next: a slippery curve,
A drop-off-the-table slider,
A mean change-up.

Scouts followed him everywhere,
And he signed for big money,
Brought him up to an A team.
But he got to drinking
After hours and especially
When his pitches went wild,
And he couldn't find the plate no more.
So he drank
His self to death.
Do you hear me?
Do you hear this story?

Reading

I don't get reading.
Some words I know,
Some I don't.
I pick up a book;
I like the cover
Because it looks exciting,
But when I try the words
I get mad.

Ms. Burns says, "Start
At the beginning of the word,
Be patient, relax."
But my whole body shakes
Wanting that word,
And it won't come to me,
So I slam the book shut
And I want to cry,
All because of those words,
Those miserable, miserable words.

Writing

Writing is easier than reading.
That's because I make the words.
I can write anything, sound it out.
I write about Sullivan,
His trip to the Vet's.
I write about poop
And the kids laugh.
Everybody knows poop;
They see it every day
On the curbs, sidewalks,
In the street.
I like to make the kids laugh,
Even Ms. Burns laughs.

Marshall @

Ms. Burns Won't Let Me Be

Ms. Burns won't let me be.
She's on my case all day long.
She says, "Focus on your work."
I try but I can't do it.
Marco wants to talk to me.
Amadeo makes a funny face.
And I get to laughing,
Again she says, "Focus."
I hate that word.
I hate doing paper work
With words I don't know.
She says, "You'll get behind."
I know I'll never catch up.
Never in a thousand years
Will I ever catch up.

Some days she's nice;
She knows about Sullivan.
I thought she'd yell when
I tripped Amadeo,
But she was quiet
And nice; she's really
Very pretty and I like
The way she smells
First thing in the morning.

Gina

Gina

I am the tallest girl
In fifth grade.
I can outrun any girl
In my room.
I proved it last spring
When we had a race,
And the boys teased
Me when I beat the girls.
So I said, okay, I'll
Race you and I won,
Beat them all.

I live on the eighteenth
Floor of our apartment
Building. Sometimes I sit
In the window and look down
At the roof gardens
That are like little parks.
I look at people through my
Binoculars and study them.

My Dad works at NBC studios
And my Mom works in marketing.
That's where they met.
They work hard so we can live
In this plush apartment
So high up.

Afternoons I go to the dance studio
Where Madame Dubois
Is very demanding.
I love to plié and jeté.
I love the feeling
In my body after a workout.

I Tell Secrets to Myself

I tell secrets to myself.
I'm a show-off.
I like people to see
Me dance, run, and jump.

I do those things
And just out of the corner
Of my eye I look
For their faces, glancing faces.
Shh, those are my secrets.

I stole the last cookie
From my little brother, Antonio.
He shouted; Mom said
I had the last one. "Fess up."
But I was very quiet
Reading my book.

I saw two people kissing
Down on the lower terrace,
Through my binoculars.
I was curious
What would happen next.
Uh oh, so I put
The binoculars down.
I don't like that secret.

I was happy
When Lanore pulled a muscle
In ballet and I got her part.
I told Lanore I was sorry,
But I was really glad.
I tell secrets to myself
That no one knows
And sometimes
I don't even
Understand myself.

℮ Gina

Horses

When we go to Central Park
I watch the horses
With their smooth, satin
Flanks, their erect,
Proud posture,
And I imagine myself
Sitting there,
holding the reins,
Wearing my black cap.
I turn my head
To catch the glances
Of friends.

I read all the horse books
In Ms. Burns' room.
I read about race horses,
Jumping horses,
Work horses. I love
Their loud smell
In the manure strewn
On the riding paths.

On my wall at home,
Above my bureau
Is a big picture
Of Smarty Jones.
I cried so hard
When he lost
The Triple Crown.
My horse, Smarty Jones.

Gina @

Madame Dubois

Madame Dubois is a tyrant,
She says, "Now you are front
Row, you perform front row."
She never saw me
When I was behind Lanore.

She counts, "One and two,
And one and two, now turn,
Not that way Gina,
We have to wait for Gina.
Again, one and two.
Practice at the bar
And mirror, Gina.
See for yourself,
Not good, not good."

I am red with tears.
Later, I practice alone,
Look for imperfection
The crook in my arm,
My chin, is it level?
The slightest flaw.

I feel sick to my stomach.
I'll ask Mom
For a bar and mirror
So I can practice at home.

Public School

We are in the ballet dressing room.
The other kids are taking
Off their monogrammed maroon jackets
And putting them on
Hangers in their lockers.

They look at me in my scruffy
Stuff, putting my favorite windbreaker
On a hook. "Is that the uniform
For public school?" Muffie asks.
She goes to private school.
Just me and another kid
Go to public school.

I don't like the tone
Of her voice when
She says public school.
It's a snotty tone
That says I'm second best.

I hear them talking
To each other as they mumble
About the hole in my tights.
And I fire right back
At them and say,
"Would you like
To race me right outside
On the street,
A real sprint?"

When I don't do the turns
To perfection I feel
Their stares and curled lips.
I hear them snickering
And see them glancing
To show me they know
And I don't. Hah!

Crying

Mom picks me up at ballet.
She asks, "So what's
Wrong? Something
Isn't right. I can tell."

"Madame Dubois."
I begin to cry.
"I can't do it.
I can't do it."

"Do what?"
"Be in the front row,
Turn correctly.
Please get me a bar
And mirror."
I cry some more
The crying is feeling good now.
I shift into big gear crying.
My nose is running,
And I'm taking big breaths,
My voice is rising.
"Please get
Me a bar and mirror!"
I watch my mother
Out of the corner of my eye.
She's frowning and looks worried.
I like to make her
Feel guilty.
Why do I do that?

@ *Gina*

Immigration

Ms. Burns says we'll study
Immigration for six weeks,
Go to Ellis Island,
Put in our family names
On the computer.
We'll do projects,
Have committees.

So, Ms. Burns puts
Me with Amadeo,
And Marco because
We're Italian. We talk
About our ancestors
What year they came,
And all about the ships.

Marco is loud and bossy;
He wants to organize us
And I won't let him.
Amadeo is shy, quiet,
And draws beautifully.

We'll go ask our parents,
And get real dates,
About when people were born,
And the places they came
From in Italy, places
With funny sounding names.

When Mom comes home
I ask when we came over
And she says I'll have
To ask your father. I tell
Her I want to go to Ellis Island
This Saturday. I want
To put in Great Grampa's
Name on the computer
But I don't even

Gina ❧

Know his name.
Dad says "I'll have to ask
My sister."

"Do it now," I beg.
"Call her right now."
Dad smiles like he understands
And gets the information,
Vittorio Bolognese, 1909.

Amadeo

Amadeo brings in sketches
He's made of old ships
That brought people to Ellis Island.
He is really good
Putting in just the right shading.

When I work on the other
Side of the room,
And turn my head
I see Amadeo's brown eyes
Staring at me.
I can even feel his eyes
On the back of my shirt.

When I turn those eyes
Are staring right at me.
I hold his eyes wondering
Why he stares, what's there,
What is fascinating him?

Kids tease us.
Amadeo loves Gina.
They don't let up with it.
Amadeo is just quiet.
I say, "Are you kidding?
He's the smallest
And I'm the tallest.
Are you kidding?"
But I don't like
The sound of my voice
When I say those things.

I Love Books

I love books,
I eat them,
Sleep them,
Dream them.

I read series books:
Lewis' Narnia,
Rowling's Harry Potter,
Henry's horse books,
Anything about horses.

When Ms. Burns reads aloud
I can see the characters,
Feel what they want.
She'll tease us with a new author,
And everyone wants that book,
So Ms. Burns raffles
The book off; she'll draw
Four new names
And that's the waiting list.
My heart pounds
To be on the waiting list.

My Mom buys me books,
And I have shelves of books
At home. I've read them all.
They are my friends
And every once in a while
I run my fingers over
The bindings and read
Them again. I dare you.
Ask me any question
About those books.

℮ *Gina*

I Write Chapter Books

I want to be a real author
So I write chapter books.
I create real characters
Right out of my head.

Right now I'm on chapter
Eighteen of a mystery.
But this book is like
Out of control.
Eliza, my main character,
Is lost in a cave
Hunting for the lost treasure.
Her flashlight battery
Has gone dead
And it is a long way
To get back out.
I wish I could think of a way.
I'll have to ask Stephanie
And if she doesn't know
I'll ask Ms. Burns.
I wonder if this ever happens
To real authors.

Gina

I Think Ms. Burns Is a Good Teacher

I know I'm a good reader
And sometimes Ms. Burns
Asks me to read aloud to the class.
She says I read with good expression.

The other day Marco
And I got in an argument
Over the best way
To organize our immigration
Project. Marco was being stupid
So Ms. Burns came over
And asked each of us
For our point of view.
Then she asked me
To tell Marco's point of view.
I hate it when she does that.

I wish she could control Marshall.
He's a big bully
Pushes everyone around
Except for me.
The other day he just exploded
For no reason.
Something about his reading book.
It took her ten minutes
To calm him down.

But she's really a good teacher;
She makes us laugh
When she told the story
About when her pet mouse
Got loose when she
Was in fifth grade like us.
Sometimes she teases us
And we have to check her smile
To know what she means.
I like Ms. Burns.

Gina

Marco

Marco

I have one sister, Dorothy.
She's skinny and two years
Younger than me.
Our family is all over New York.
I have a zillion cousins
In Queens, Brooklyn
But I live in Manhattan
Where my Dad is a dentist.

I'm a Yankee fan like my Dad,
But all my cousins in Queens
Are Mets fans. We argue
So much we almost fight.
"Hah," I say, "So what's
Your pitching going to do
Against Jeter, Giambi, Sheffield
A-Rod and Posada?"

We have big dinners.
When the Yanks play the Mets.
It is wild when we are together.
But a lot of fun too.
Mom starts cooking sauce
And meatballs the week before
We go to Queens.
All week long the smell
Reminds me of the series
We are going to win.

Dad expects me to do good
In school. I get a B
And he's on my case.

"Let me see your papers,"
He says, and he goes over
Every little thing.
"This spelling, atrocious,
This science paper,
Pure carelessness."
I get an A.
He says, "That's what
You are supposed to get."

Marco

My Sister Dorothy

My sister Dorothy is in third grade
And is a pain in the butt.
She's always squawking
Like the other day
When me and Dad went
To the Yankees ball game
She squawked and squawked
Because he only had two tickets.
I just wanted it to be me and Dad.

Dad said to Dorothy
"I'll take you anywhere
You want but I can't
Take you today."
That didn't stop her.
She said, "I like A-Rod
And I want to see him."
Then she started to cry.
It was awful.
I felt a little sorry for her.

But not when she goes
Into my room without permission,
When she takes one of my CD's
Or one of my computer games
She just does it.
No apologies.
Sometimes I give her a slap
And then she really yells,
Cries all the way to Mom
Or Dad if he's home.
Then I get grounded
Because she took my CD.
I don't get it.

Marco ☺

Yankee Stadium

Me and Dad went
To a Yankees/Red Sox game.
I wore my Derek Jeter shirt
And my Yankees hat.

First we got a program
With pictures of the ball players.
When we walked up the runway
I asked Dad for an ice cream
But he said to wait
Until we got our seats.

Suddenly the runway
Opened up and there was the field,
The greenest field ever.
With a brown infield, white foul lines,
And the sounds of smacking baseballs.

We sat right behind the Yankee
Dugout and right away
I saw Derek Jeter,
A-Rod, and Giambi.

Dad says Yankee/Red Sox games
Are special because the crowd
Has a different sound
Like an all the time roar.

The best day ever,
Me and my Dad.
Of course
The Yankees won.

@ *Marco*

Pictures from the Past

I spoke with Mom
And she said I could bring
The suitcase full of Ellis
Island stuff, but she'd
Have to be there with me.

I asked Ms. Burns could
I show the class some immigration stuff
And she said yes.
I opened my great, great
Grandfather's case with the snap
Locks, reached in and pulled
Out his picture,
And then I showed the ship
He came on
With four smoke stacks.

"How long was the ship?"
Asked Marshall. "How many people
Did it carry?" Asked Rueben.
I said, "This isn't about the ship;
This is about my great, great grandfather.
This is his picture.
Here is his little passport booklet.
See it is all stamped up.
I got another photo.
These are the clothes
They wore way back then.
You know you could get
Sent back to Italy
If you had an eye problem
Or you coughed bad."
"He didn't get sent back
Did he?" Asked Gina.
I said, "I wouldn't
Be here if he did."
The class laughed. Gina didn't.

Immigration

Ms. Burns wants us to study
Immigration. She put Gina,
Amadeo, and me together
Because we're Italians.
She said we can help
Each other, divide
Up the project.

So, right away Gina
Wants to take charge,
Like she wants to be the boss.
I say, "So what name
You gonna look up?" She's stuck
And can't come up with one.
I say, "I already have
A name, Marco Agostini,
My great, great grandfather."
She wants me and Amadeo
To get on the computer first
And I say, "I don't need
To, I already know."

Well, things get loud
And Ms. Burns asks
Me for my point of view,
And then what's Gina's.
I can say Gina's point of view,
But she can't say mine.
Ms. Burns says, "I'll
Be back in fifteen minutes
And I want this settled."

So Amadeo hasn't said anything
Yet and he says, "Why don't I
Do the family thing,
Because I have good stuff already,
And Gina can get on the net."
Amadeo wants to draw people
Looking up at the Statue
Of Liberty from their ship.
Amadeo says, "How's that?" I said,
"Sounds good to me."
Gina says, "Oh all right,"
And huffs off to the computer.

Going to the Doctor

I don't like doctors
They give you shots.
When I was in second grade
I cut myself on a can
So I got a shot
With a humungous needle.

Now I'm going
Because I have a pain
In my stomach.
It hurts and aches
When I reach up
Or bend over.

Mom is worried
So I'm in Dr. Vintaglia's office
And the nurse asks
Me and my mom questions.
I don't like the smell in there.

Dr. Vintaglia says, "Get your pants
Down and lie right here
On the table so I can check you."
I wish the nurse would leave.

The doctor blows on his hands.
"Got to warm these up"
He says with a laugh.
I don't understand what he means.

"This may hurt because I'm going
To push. Raise your hand
If it hurts too much."
So the doctor goes to work
Pushing around the sore spot.

Marco

"I think he has a pulled muscle,"
He says to mom. "But I find
No mass or anything.
We'll take x-rays
To be sure. I'll be back
To you if we find anything.
Just rest and aspirin."

At least I didn't get a shot.

Andy

Andy and I
Do everything together
Like Little League.
He's a pitcher; I'm the catcher.
We both like the Yankees
So he pretends he's Mike Mussina
And I'm Jorge Posada.

In the afternoon
Andy comes over to my house
To play Nintendo games.
Today we've chosen
Return of the Joker
And we have to get good
At using a grappling hook.
To fight the Joker
And we have to keep fighting
Until he is dead.

Mom doesn't like the game.
Because she says I don't like
You killing people.
We say, "It's only make believe.
It's only fun."
We end up quitting
The game anyway.

Mostly Andy and me
Like to design
The ultimate game,
A medieval game
With knights, kings
Castles, catapults
Moats and disasters.
We draw it out
On big sheets of paper.
Andy and I
Can play for hours
And forget about
Everything else.

Marco

I Like to Read History Books

Lloyd Alexander is my favorite author.
I like to read books
About other times.
Alexander takes me back
To castles and wars.
His detail is magnificent.

But I like books
About the Civil War too,
Books like *The Red Badge of Courage*.
My Dad said he read it in college
In Freshman English.
I think he's impressed
That I am reading it too.
That makes me feel good.
I follow the Southern generals
Who outsmarted
The Northern Generals left and right.

I follow the Civil War on maps
From a book by Bruce Catton
Where he showed pictures
Of the battles and the maneuvers
Of North and South.
Mostly I look at the pictures.
I love that stuff,
The strategy stuff, that Lee did.

I read *Johnny Tremain*
About this kid in the Revolution,
Who works with Paul Revere
But hurts his hand,
And works for the *Observer*
To deliver pamphlets.
I want to be like Tremain
And do something
For my Country.

Marco @

I Like to Write Chapter Books

Me and Andy, I mean
Andy and I.
My Dad is always
Correcting me
On that one,
Like to write chapter books.

Ms. Burns gave us permission
To write a book together
And we've been writing
It for two months now.
It is a book that follows
Two brothers our age
Who live in the south
Who spot a northern
Maneuver to outflank
The Rebels in the Wilderness
Campaign. We have
The battle plan on a map
And we've located
Their house and how
They let Lee know.

Every once in a while
We share our story so far.
The kids keep asking
When are you going
To read another chapter?

Ms. Burns says
It is all about character
And not just the war.
So we go back to work
And ask who
Are these brothers anyway?
What do they want?
That's what real authors do
When they write chapter books.

@ *Marco*

Ms. Burns Is Cool

Ms. Burns is cool.
She keeps an eye out
For history books
For kids my age,
But she knows I can
Read tougher books
About history.

One day she shocked me
When she said
The entire Yankee lineup
Including all the starting pitchers
And the bullpen.
I asked her
How did she know that?
Since she was six years old
She followed the Yanks
With her Dad.
She showed me
How to score a game
On a piece of paper.

She laughs a lot
But if you don't do your work,
She's on your case
Like my father.
Ms. Burns is cool.

Stacy

Stacy

I wish I didn't have to go
To school, or have anything
To do with it. The girls pick
On me and I don't like
The way they look at me
Or whisper behind my back.

I'd just like to disappear,
Be invisible.
My nose is too big, my hair
Never looks good.
My teeth are crooked.
I'm too heavy.
I wish I was thinner
But I eat too much
Of my own sweet stuff.
If I am not cooking
I watch TV.

My sister, Imelda, is nice
To me and she's in 9th grade.
She is beautiful and wears
The latest makeup.
Boys are always calling
Her up on the telephone.

I like it when Ms. Burns
Reads to us but when I read
I don't know all the words.
And then I get sleepy and hungry
Just having to do the reading papers
Which are so boring.

My mom says I've got a reading
Problem and I need extra help.
I know I've got a problem
But nobody does anything
About it. I mean nobody,
'Cept maybe Ms. Burns
Who helps a little
But doesn't have the answers.

I Love to Bake

I love to bake,
Especially cakes,
Muffins, rolls, cookies,
Sweet stuff. When I get
Home from school
I already know what I want
To eat and I can read recipes,
Because I get the measures
Right, three cups of flour,
One cup of sugar,
Shortening, baking powder.
I know those words
And I'm good at math,
Good at measuring.

My sister Imelda doesn't cook.
She's always on a diet.
Not me. I call Rosalie
Who lives down
On the second floor.
She's in third grade
And likes to cook with me.
I say, "Come on up and cook."

Today we'll make a hot milk cake.
I'm teaching her how to cook.
So, we put on aprons,
And lay out measuring cups,
Spoons, salt, sugar, flour, milk.
I read and I watch Rosalie
Measure three cups of flour.
She does it very carefully.

When we finish putting
On the chocolate frosting
We've got a great cake
That Mom likes to eat.
She says, "With you in the house
Who needs to buy
Pastries at the grocery store
Or at the bakery?"

Stacy

Mom

Mom divorced Dad
Five years ago
When I was little.
It was pretty messy
I don't know the details.

Mom is working two jobs.
She does computer work until 4:00,
Comes home about 4:30,
Then leaves at 6:00
To be a cocktail waitress.
She says she makes
More money as a cocktail waitress.
She says if we want this apartment
She's got to work,
All there is to it,
she's got to work.

I really wish she could be here,
To see me bake my cakes,
To help me with my reading.
This place is just boring.
All I have is the TV.
And Imelda.

Imelda is on the phone
With boys, and I can tell
By her talk, she's up to no good.
She slips out of the house,
Says, Be back in an hour.
Sometimes it's two hours.
She bribes me not to tell Mom.
One time she came
In with a big bruise
On her cheek.
I worry about Imelda.

Stacy ❦

Immigration

We are studying immigration
Before we go to Ellis Island.
So I'm in a dumb group
Of kids with Ricky Fuentes,
And Vicky Sanchez.
Ms. Burns put me there
Because of my Puerto Rican
Father's name, Menendez.
We are supposed
To trace our ancestors.

After the divorce my Mom
Went back to her name from home
Which is Robinson.
I asked her could we change
Our name too? She said she
Didn't have the money.
So, I'm stuck
With Vicky who doesn't like me,
And Ricky who really wants
To know where he came from.

Ricky talked to his Mom and Dad
And he says his grandparents
Came in the sixties, forty years ago.
He says they came from Ponce
And they used to work
In the sugar cane fields.

Vicky says she talked to her Mom
And her Mom says she doesn't know,
Maybe San Juan. So, we're stuck.
Ricky has stuff and Vicky and I don't.
We call Ms. Burns and she asks,
"What do you have so far?
What's your solution so far?"

Stacy

Solutions

Ms. Burns asks,
"What have you done so far?"
Ricky says, "I have good stuff;
We're from Ponce."
Vicky says, "I got nothing."
I say, "I don't want
To be Puerto Rican."

Ricky's eyes get wide like
He can't figure me out.
Vicky puffs her chest
And says, "What's wrong
With that? You ashamed?"
I say, "It's complicated" and I can feel
The tears coming.

"Wait a minute," says Ms. Burns,
"Stacy, I'll speak with you alone,
But I want you all
To use the tools like the Internet
To find out more.
Put your last name
On the Net and see what's there.
Look in the telephone book
And count how many
Named Sanchez or Fuentes.
I think you'll get
A good surprise."

When we're alone
She says, "What's on your mind, Stacy?"
"I want to be Robinson like Mom.
I don't want to be Puerto Rican."
She says, "I'm sorry I put you
In a tough spot.
I want you to at least check
Menendez and then
Ask Mom for background

On Robinson. I want you,
Ricky, and Vicky
To get along and help
Each other with resources.
Can you do that?"
She looks me in the eye
When she asks that.
I say, "Okay, I'll do it."

Imelda

Imelda and I are close
Because we have
So much time together.
She's real thin,
Wears tight clothes,
And classy jewelry.
I like the way she does
Her hair. She treats me
Like a sister her age.

I told her about
Not wanting
To be Puerto Rican.
Her face looked like Ricky's.
She asked why
And I told her I wanted
To be Robinson, not Menendez.

Our Dad was not a bad man.
He and Mom were just
So different they couldn't get along.
You were too young
And couldn't remember
The good things.
He used to cook
For us, take us to the Park,
Buy us little presents.
He loved us.
I'd give anything
To see him again.
He just disappeared.

I Wish I Could Read Better

I like math.
I don't like reading.
I like the numbers,
I can do a line of addition
Or subtraction as fast
As anyone in this room.

I can read picture books,
Especially the ones
That are about science,
Or animals.
But it takes me a long time
To get the words right.
I wish I was faster.

I go down to the reading center
Where Ms. Savitsky
Helps me with the words,
Look at the picture clues,
Look at the other words
To make sense.
I guess I'm a little better
Than before, but I don't
Think I will ever catch up.

We have reading tests
That get timed.
I feel sick to my stomach
And I have a head ache.
Everyone is doing the test
But I can't concentrate.
I read but I don't remember
It because I'm so nervous.
I know I'll get a low score.
I know I won't pass.
The other girls ask
"How did you do?
How did you do?"
I say, "Shut up.
It's none of your business."

@ *Stacy*

I Don't Have Much to Say

I don't have much to say.
Mostly I'm quiet in class.
When I write
I write about food,
My baking,
My sister, Imelda,
Or TV.

My writing is blah.
I can get the words down
Pretty well, but who
Would be interested
In anything I write?

I hate sharing.
I get cold in my fingers
And hot in my face.
I feel it in my stomach
Because the bad three:
Vicky, Andrea, and Tracy
Are looking at me,
Making faces, snickering
And asking stupid questions.
Rebekah tries to help
And Ms. Burns tries
To help. She addresses
The class saying, "Look
For the good parts."
But I know I'm not
A good writer.
I just know it.
I don't have much to say.

Stacy @

My Friend, Rebekah

She isn't really my friend.
Rebekah is everybody's friend.
So, she's not a special, special friend
Like Rosalie who I cook with;
Know what I mean?

When Rebekah sits next to me in music
I feel proud that she is really there.
Sometimes she sits across
From me at lunch
And says, "Want to eat
One of my cookies?"

Rebekah is smart like Gina,
But like most of the time
She says just the right
Thing like "Wish I could do
Math examples like you."
To make someone
Feel good. I don't have
The words to say
What she does.
She's just nice.
Know what I mean?

Stacy

Ms. Burns

Ms. Burns is a nice teacher.
She's friendly and helps everybody.
Mostly I just keep quiet.
When Marshall gets loud
Or upset I sort
Of shrink in my seat.
I just get out of the way.

Sometimes Marshall really gets
To Ms. Burns and she can't
Take it any more
And she yells at him
To stop it this minute.
The class gets very quiet
At times like that.

I can tell she wishes
I could read better.
When I'm reading
And writing answers
To questions, I slug it out.

I wish she'd just leave
Me alone. I try to cover
My paper with my hand.
I look like I'm working
Very hard, but really I'm not.

She likes the way
I do math. I whip
Down the rows
Like lightning.
I can do numbers
In my head. She says,
If you could relax
in reading, the way
you do in math,
you'd be a good reader.
She acts like I'm smart.
Maybe I am.

Stacy @

Amadeo

Amadeo

I am the smallest kid in my class.
I don't like it that I am small
Because I get picked on,
Beat up, and I always
Have to be watching
To protect myself.
I'm keeping a look out
For Marshall; I need
To know where he is
All the time.

Ms. Burns says she likes
My art. She took down
One of my water colors
And said, "This has to have
A nice blue backing."
She surprised me.

I love art.
I sketch, paint, draw
All the time. But my big brother
Takes my work, marks it up,
Or tosses it in the waste basket.
He calls me rodent,
Pip-squeak, and punches me.

But I have my ways
To get him when he's out.
I hide his toothbrush,
His favorite jacket,
They just disappear
And I play dumb.

My Dad left two years ago,
Just took off,
And we haven't seen him since.
Mom does the best
She can with two jobs.
But it's hell around here
Being stuck at home
With my wicked brother.

The Metropolitan

Our class took a field trip
To the Metropolitan
And we were supposed
To have partners but I gave
Mine the slip
And I wandered on my own
Through all the rooms:
The Egyptians, the Greeks
And Romans. I studied
The vases, the clean lines,
The simple constructions.
I just lost myself in art,
And Ms. Burns was some upset
At me. I'm sorry I did that
But I'm not sorry
I saw all that art.

So now I'm giving my brother
The slip, getting out
Of our apartment and going
Back to the Metropolitan.
It is ten blocks down
And five city blocks over.
I memorized it when
We went. I can't get in
But I just love looking at
The building, walking
Through the art, the colors,
The street vendors
Are selling.
I wander through the store.
Some day I'll have enough
Money to buy
My own ticket
And stay all day
If I feel like it.

@ *Amadeo*

Marshall

Marshall always has his hands
On someone, or is pushing them.
He's the biggest kid
In the room
So no one stands up to him.

Today I could tell he was upset.
He went after me,
Gave me a shove,
Tried to trip me, and Ms. Burns
Saw it all and said, "You two,
Over here." I wanted her
To bawl him out,
Tell him to leave me alone.
But she spoke quiet,
"Marshall, your Granny
told me about your Dog."

I was surprised to see tears
Come into his eyes.
He said his dog, Sullivan,
Is at the Vet's and they don't know
What's wrong with him,
Marshall just looked at the floor.
And I saw more tears.
Ms. Burns waited for
Marshall to talk.
I waited a long time too
And then I said, "I had a dog
Once, a mutt and he
Was killed in the street
Where we used to live.
His name was Lightning."

Marshall looked at me
Like he understood
And asked, "So did you
Get another one?"
I said, "No, we moved
And we can't have a dog
Where we live now."
The bell rang for recess.

Gina

We are studying immigration
So Ms. Burns put Gina, Marco,
And me in one group.
Marco and Gina argue
Over how we'll do it.
They don't even want
To know what I think.

We talk about ships
That bring the immigrants over.
I see pictures of the people
Lining the rails and waving.
So I draw the ship fast
Using the charcoal edge
To give an impression
Of the ship and the people.

We come together
The next day and Gina
Said, "I like the feel
Of this charcoal."

She sees my charcoal
And she says nice things
About it. "I can't
Put my finger on
What it is, but
We can use this."
No girl ever said
Nice things about anything
I ever did in my art.

I look at Gina again,
Like for the first time
And notice how beautiful
She is, her smile

And brown hair.
She is so tall
And I am so short.

I watch her;
I watch everything she does.
She picks up a book
And I want the title,
So I can read it too.
The other day I was staring
And she turned and looked
At me in a long-look way.
I wondered what
She was thinking.
I do that a lot now,
Look right at her
Hoping she'll look back.
Kids tease me and say,
"You love Gina."
They say it again
And again. I suppose
I do but Gina keeps saying,
"Are you kidding?
Are you kidding?"
But I don't think
She really means that.

Amadeo

My Brother, Angelo

Something is wrong with my brother.
He's in eighth grade,
And most of the time he is angry.
He bangs things,
Gives me shoves.
I try to stay out of his way,
But that's just about impossible.
There's just the two of us,
Every afternoon.

He has homework
But he doesn't do it.
Mom is really on his case
Because he's failing.
He says he doesn't care.
Once I came home early
And Angelo was crying.

He really beat me up
That time. I got out
Of the house just in time.
Later I told Mom
About getting beat up,
My bloody nose
And black eye.
She shook her head
And sighed.
"What am I going to do?
What am I going to do?"
Well, I wish she'd
Do something.
I'm getting killed.

A Visit to Marshall's Apartment

I didn't want to go.
Marshall's grandmother reached
My mother and Mom said,
"You need to get out of here.
So Saturday you are going."

I said, "He pushes me
And whacks me like Angelo."
"His Grandma said Marshall
Has a dog he wants
You to see. Remember
How you felt so bad
When Lightning was killed?
So give it a try.
I'll go with you."

So we went
And Mom knocked on the door.
I hid behind Mom and felt scared.
Marshall said, "My dog
Is bigger than you."
But he must have seen
The look on my face,
Cuz he said, "Oh he's just
A big dog." But Sullivan
Looked so friendly and happy
To see me I got down
And asked him for his paw.
Sullivan just looked at me.
I said "Sit" like I used to do
With Lightning, and Sullivan
Just looked at me stupid like.

I said "Sit" and pushed his back down.
I did it again and again
Until he finally did it,
And then I asked for his paw
Again and again until he did that too.
I said, "See, you've got a smart dog."
And Marshall had such a big smile.
We had a good time after that.

@ *Amadeo*

The Art Show

Ms Burns says there's an Art Show
And part of the show is a contest.
She urges me to send in one of my pieces.
My pieces are safe in school.
I search and search my portfolio
Trying to decide, trying to think
Back to the Metropolitan
With all the paintings and art objects.
I wait for one of mine to hit me,
One to turn a head, make
The judge come back.

I choose one I did in Central Park.
A rock, a bench, a lone tree,
With buildings showing themselves
Above the trees, above the noise
A quiet, peaceful place in the city.

The next day the class
Goes to the park, to the show,
To where the judges have decided.
I go to my painting and it isn't
Where I saw it yesterday.
Someone has stolen it.
But Ms. Burns says,
"Come with me."
She has a tear in her eye.
We walk to the center
Of the fence,
And there is mine
With a blue ribbon,
It reads, "Grand Prize, Best of Show."
Nothing like this
Has ever happened
In my whole life.

My Thoughts About Reading

Gary Paulsen is my author.
He creates such wonderful pictures
When he writes, the picture
Of the camp site in *Hatchet*,
The picture of pissing
In *Harris and Me*. I thought
I'd wet my own pants laughing
During that story.

Sometimes when I walk
In Central Park I see trees
Rocks and bushes
And I change them to Alaska
Or the Iditarod with the dogs
Running and I think of Lightning
And Sullivan with me
As they race through the snow.
Sometimes I just can't stop
My mind from seeing those places.

The other day Ms. Burns read,
The Man Who Walked Between the Towers.
It was a great story
But what got me was how the artist
Kept changing perspectives
Between the man,
The towers and the ground.
I couldn't wait to try it myself.

I love reading. It just sends
My imagination to other places.

@ Amadeo

I'm Not Really a Writer

I'm not really a writer.
Gina's a writer; Rebekah's a writer
Because they write chapter books.
They turn out pages and pages
And I don't know how they do it.

Gina says, "I'm on page 18
What page are you on?"
And Rebekah says, "Page 16."
I never write more
Than a page and a half.

I write about Lightning,
The Park and Alaska.
And after a page I can't
Think of any more to write.

Mostly I write to illustrate
What I've written.
I drew Lightning
And took a long time doing it.
Every detail had
To be just right:
The head, the nose, the eyes.
I wrote about Alaska
So I could think
Of being right there,
But that was only a page.
I'm not really a writer.

My Teacher Is Proud of Me

I remember when Ms. Burns
Said she wanted to put some blue
Backing on my water color.
She really liked my work.

But when we went
To the Metropolitan
I just didn't want
To be with my partner,
So I gave him the slip
And saw the museum
All by myself. I got lost
A little and Ms. Burns
Went frantic with worry.
She just shook her head
Like she expected me
To do that. She had tears
And finally a smile.

I guess she knew my work
Was special. She told me
To enter the show
But respected me
To make the best choice
Of my stuff for the show.

I'll never forget the time
When I saw tears in her eyes,
And she just stood there
Not moving or anything.
I just know she was proud
When I won the prize.
It was a special time and feeling
For both of us.

Amadeo

Rebekah

Rebekah

My brother, Aaron,
Is almost thirteen,
Attends Hebrew school
On Saturdays, to prepare
For his Bar Mitzvah.
Aaron is very serious,
Working hard to memorize
His prayer in Hebrew

Poppa owns three delicatessens.
He says, "Honor the help
And they will honor you
With good service
To the customers.
Customers like a friendly face
And good food"; that's what
Poppa says all the time.

Mama helps in the delis.
She has sharp eyes and good ears.
She is always saying
To the help,
No to this and yes
To that
She says, "Taste this,
You'll never forget it.
Customers have choices.

They can go to other Delis
So give good helpings,
And smile a lot."

The Violin

I was three years old
When mother took
Me to my first Suzuki lesson.
It was a very good experience
As I watched the older
Kids play and I got
My first Suzuki violin.

Mother was always there as
I listened and listened
To Mendelssohn's violin music.
Then standing there stroking
The bow with the instrument tucked
Under my chin and playing
the music as best I could.
And it all sounded so good
Even when I was learning.

I learned technique watching
The others play, took little
Short passages and worked
On them. Our master, Mr. Bernstein,
Was always encouraging.
He said it is like learning
To talk, just watch and play,
Feel the music.

It is now seven years
Later. I am able
To read music, play
In an orchestra.
I practice, practice
Just to have fun.
Know what?
I have so many friends
At Suzuki, two of them,
Adelaide and Masha
Were there

Rebekah

When I first started.
We say, "Let's have fun
And practice together."
We change our clothes
So we're loose,
Get out our violins,
Decide what to play
Stroke away and move
Our fingers in stirring
Vibratos.

One Day

One day, five years ago,
When the fire engines
Were screaming in the streets
And smoke was in the air,
I heard about the terrorists
Who drove planes
Into the twin towers.

I asked Mom
"Who did that?"
And she said, "There are people
Who hate us,
Who hate our country."

I asked her,
"Do they hate me?"
"No, they don't hate you,
They just hate us
All together."

We talked about it
At school; it was on the radio,
On TV, and I still wonder
What we did
To make them so angry,
That they'd give their lives
Just to punish us.

When I go to bed
I wonder what
I have done wrong
To bring so much hate.

ⓔ *Rebekah*

Stacy

The girls tease Stacy
Because she's not pretty,
Or maybe because she's just quiet.
Or maybe because
It's just fun to see
If she'll cry.

Sometimes Ms. Burns
Doesn't know they do that.
I try to sit next to Stacy
At lunch. We talk
And she tells me
About her cooking
After school. I say,
"Would you come
Watch them cook
At my Poppa's Deli?
Ask your Mom."
"I've got an extra chocolate
Chip cookie in my lunch.
Would you like one?"

My Best Friend, Masha

Masha is my best friend,
We go to Hebrew school,
We play the violin
But she goes to private school.
No matter, after school
We talk on the telephone,
We talk about everything,
CD's, maybe boys;
She's into boys
More than I am.

We are both reading,
Harry Potter, we burn
Through all the Harry
Potter books. It's like
We enter a new country,
The Hogwarts School,
Oh how I wish I could
Write like Rowlings.

But Masha's parents
Fight and try to put
Her in the middle
By confiding little things
Like going shopping
Or maybe getting her
A new violin, a ring,
But her parents
Don't tell each other the details
And it is terribly upsetting
To her. She's afraid
They might get a divorce.
But I tell her
She'll always have
Me for a friend.
Even if she moves away
We'll have our cell phones
We can send e-mail
And pictures of each other.

Nothing can separate us
Because we are best friends.

Rebekah

Stories We'll Never Forget

Friday night we always
Have dinner together.
Nothing else can happen
To take us away.

After prayers and eating
Sometimes there will be a story.
Last Friday Poppa told
How his great grandfather, Samuel,
Escaped the Russian pogroms,
Got on a ship, landed in New York
At Ellis Island in 1905,
Worked the docks,
Met his wife Anna,
Who worked as a stitcher,
Lower East side.
They had nothing
But love to keep them going,
Mind you, they started
With nothing but love.
I hear Poppa repeating
It again and again,
Nothing but love.

I like it when Poppa
Leans back in his chair,
Clears his throat
And begins to talk
In his deep bass voice.

Mama waits until he finishes
And then she begins
To tell her stories.

I think it is beautiful
To just listen to family stories.

Poor Marshall

When Marshall blows up
The rest of the room
Gets very quiet,
Unless he's in an argument
With some kid,
And then there's the two
Of them pushing
And shoving each other.

I wait until it is over
And then I speak
To him quietly.
I've seen Mama
Talk to customers
Who have had a bad day.

He is still shaking,
And I ask him,
"Are you okay?
Can I get you something?
Can I read
A story to you?
You choose; I'll read."

Mostly his head is down,
And he's talking to himself.
Eventually he looks
At me and says,
"The baseball book,
The one about the Yankees,
Read to me from that one."
Sometimes he wants
Me to show him
The players' names,
So he can remember them.

@ *Rebekah*

Fantasy

Time flies when I read.
I look up at the clock;
An hour has gone by.
Each character.
I want what they want
Except for the bad guys.

Ms. Burns has a new
System where I need three
Books. So I choose
An easy nature book
With many pictures.
I realize I can learn lots
From this book on bears,
How they have their young
In January when asleep.

For the level I am on now
I'll just continue with anything
J. K. Rowling, or C. S. Lewis writes.

My challenge books
Will be *Lord of the Rings*.
These are long ones,
Sort of like Rowling's
Because they are imaginary
With good against evil.
The vocabulary is challenging
So I have a dictionary
Right on my desk.

Ms. Burns wants us to write
A short letter each day
To show what we are thinking,
What struck you and why.
That's hard.

Sometimes Writing Is Hard

I like to write.
Mostly I write chapter books,
But the other day
I decided to write Poppa's
Story about our family.

I tried and tried
To tell his story
About how Samuel
Came to America
And was successful,
But I only had half
A page of writing.

Ms. Burns tried to help.
She said, "You have
Sentences that are whole
Stories. You have
Plenty of time. Interview
Your father, get the real
Details about Ellis Island,
That's one story,
Then working the docks,
That's another story.
I've heard your father
Is an excellent story teller.
He'll have the details.
For now think of some
Questions you want
To ask him beginning
With the trip over,
Or Ellis Island."

Yes, this is much
More difficult
Than writing fiction books,
Because it really happened.

@ *Rebekah*

Ms. Burns Challenges Us

Ms. Burns challenges us
In reading, math, she'll say
"I don't know if you are ready
For this in math," and she'll
Toss out a real problem
From our everyday lives.

The other day she read
From *Lord of the Rings*.
She said, "See if you
Can understand this.
It may be hard."
She reads to us every day
For about ten minutes,
The stories or facts
Could be easy or hard.
If it is easy she asks
A hard question,
Or an easy one when
The reading is difficult.

Mostly, she's a lot of fun
When we have choral speaking,
We follow her voice and mouth
As she shows the words.
She conducts and we follow
With our ears. It's amazing
How we are a chorus
In about five minutes.
Or she asks us
How we'd solve a problem
And she lets us make our tries.
She says sometimes
You have to be ridiculous,
Let your mind go,
If you want to really
Solve the problem.

Rebekah ❦

The other day
She helped me when
I was writing my Dad's story.
She sends us off on special
Assignments and I learned
Lots from my Dad I didn't know.
Everyone has a job
And if we all pull together
Things are good here.
I like to help.
I like Ms. Burns.

@ *Rebekah*

Ms. Burns

Ms. Burns

I teach fifth grade at PS 142
In Manhattan. I've been there
For ten years now.
What can I say?
Most days I love teaching.
I like most of the children.
I love how different
They can be and I try
To celebrate their differences.

Some children like Marshall
Push me pretty hard.
I can feel a showdown coming
And I know he needs space.
I have to anticipate
Beyond what he can sense
And give him a gentle nudge.

Teaching is like that,
Creating appointments for learning,
Steering here, steering there,
Creating a new song
For children to sing together,
Helping the children
To pull together
And feel like a class.
Choral speaking helps,
Everyone has chores
To make this room work.

Now that takes time.
Sometimes we're a class
In September,
But more likely
Not until October.
And with tough ones
Maybe December.

I'm married and have
A ten-year-old son, Paul,
Who loves to read
Historical fiction,
And play video games.
I wish he had more friends
So he wouldn't be bored.
We live in a two bedroom
Apartment on the West Side.
We have a hard time
Making our budget work.
If Paul had an injury,
Or a physical problem
We just couldn't hack it.

@ Ms. Burns

The Children I Take Home with Me

My husband, Mark, says
When I close my door
In the afternoon
I should forget the class,
Forget the children.

I try to explain
That I can't keep
My worlds separated.
Maybe it is because
I am a woman.
I think about our son, Paul,
When I am in school.
Did he read the note
I put in his lunch box?

But mostly I carry Marshall,
On the days when he explodes.
He thunders and bellows.
It could be during reading,
A slight from another child.
I have my tender days,
With him when
He wants to help.
Mostly I wonder
What clues will unlock
His reading problem.
I am always looking
For any angle.
He is one big mystery.

I carry Amadeo
That sweet little kid;
I feel like the mother protector.
I know I can't be his mother.
But it is just my way.
The other day he came
In with a black eye
And a bruise on his cheek.

I've seen these before.
There has to be
An investigation.

I carry Stacy.
I can't put my finger
On what ails her.
She seemed very testy
About her immigration study
Which isn't her usual way.
Stacy hangs back,
Doesn't like to be noticed.
I need to learn more.

My husband says I work too hard;
He doesn't know the half of it.

@ Ms. Burns

Choices

Thursday night Paul had a slight fever,
Was it a sign of things to come?
Did he have a cold coming on?
How did he feel in his joints?
Were many absent
In his classroom at school?
I talk to him quietly,
Occasionally reach
To touch his forehead.

I spoke with my husband.
Did he have an important meeting?
Could he stay home from work?
The trip to Ellis Island on Monday
Needed more preparation.
All permission slips weren't in.
Could I give the preparation to a sub?

Mark thought
We could split the day.
He'd take the afternoon
And I'd take the morning
If Paul's condition was worse.

In the morning.
Paul felt better,
He didn't have a fever
And his eyes were more bright.
But my husband and I
Have these discussions
At least two times a month.

We Have All Come from Somewhere

We have all come
From somewhere.
There are stories
In our names.
In our families.

I ask the children
To bring in photos or memorabilia,
To look in our big telephone book
Just to see how many people
Have their same name.

I send them to the Net
To put in their last name
So they can investigate
Famous people.
Maybe there is a connection.
Who knows what they'll find?

I call all my children
By their first name
By the end of the first day.
Then I begin to write down
What is special about each one.
I carry their names in my head
And as I go through the list
I think of some good thing,
Some one thing, that each child knows
That is unique or wonderful.

Ms. Burns

Organized—Disorganized

My class is organized,
My home is disorganized.
The dishes are in the sink,
The laundry on the couch,
Papers everywhere.

Don't come to my house
Unless you call in advance.
You can come to my classroom
Any old time.

Every child in the room
Has a job to do every day
And I say, if you see a job
That needs doing don't wait,
Just do it, right then.

I show children how to read
Their work through mini-lessons;
Before papers come in
It is their job to go over them,
Check with a friend,
Write at the top
What you tried
That was new.
Sometimes Marshall doesn't care,
But when he does care
I really push him.
I noticed that he cares
More about writing
About the Yankees.

Books, science materials,
Art materials, listening center,
All have their special setups
And I know who cares for them

As the jobs rotate.
With one glance
I can tell what is out of place.

My special forte is being artful,
If I don't look out
My classroom ends
Up looking like a supermarket.
Sometimes I stop and catch myself
Crates, folders, a mess
So I reduce the distractions
To highlight children's work.
That's the ultimate organization,
The children caring
About the feel of the room.

Ms. Burns

How I Teach Writing

Some of my girls
Get stuck writing chapter books
And can't stop.
So I push them,
What does your main
Character want and want badly.
I interview them
To see how well
They know their
Main character.
Sometimes they don't
Know their character.
It's all plot.

Rebekah switched to writing
Her father's story,
Felt no flow,
Until I could show her
Where all the stories were.

I work on essays
From letters; the food
In the cafeteria.
I say, "Write a letter,
'the pizza was flat,
the fish smelly.'"
I say, "Write your position
With three good reasons
Then send the letter
To Mrs. Carver in the cafeteria.
Invite her to class
For an interview."

So I ask them
Do you have both sides
Of the question?
They groan and suffer a bit
As they keep working.
I expect a lot of them
Because these kids are smart.

Ms. Burns @

Taking a Risk

I pulled the children
Over to the rug
And chatted with them
About my approach
To reading.

I want you to be reading
Three kinds of books,
An easy book,
A regular book where you
Feel comfortable, and then
A challenge book,
You could say, "I dream of
The day I can read
That book."

You like the easy book
And you just get
The feeling of turning
The pages quickly.
What's easy and what's
Hard depends on what
You know about the subject.
I'd like to see a better balance
Between fiction and nonfiction.

So, I want you to look
Over what you've read
And list what's easy, regular,
And most difficult.
Just rate them.
Of course, I'll do the same
For the books I've read
At home and right along with you.
I'll talk about them tomorrow.

@ Ms. Burns

My Principal

As you can tell
I have an excellent principal
Who isn't intimidated
By what I do, or the flexibility
He sees me take with curriculum.

My children score well
So he turns a blind eye
To how the children get there.
He knows where
The line is drawn in the sand.
He stays on one side
And I stay on the other.

But he also knows
How to ask tough questions.
"I see you are spending
Lots of time on this play.
How do you justify the time?"
So I show him how much
Curriculum is covered
And what it does
For the children's confidence.

We do battle over tests.
I ask him, "What
Are the tests for:
The children, the teacher
Or the central administration?
What can you do
With the data except
Say, he got a ten, then what?"

He's a good man just the same.
He's on the playground
Shooting baskets
With Marshall and Gina.

Reading and Writing

I'm passing out journals
In which I want
You to write letters
About what you are reading.
I will be writing letters
About what I am reading.

I'll share my letters with you,
You'll share your letters
With me and with
A special pen pal.

Say a little bit about what the book
Is about, like *Hatchet*.
"*Hatchet* is about a kid whose plane
Crashes and he tries to survive."
Write how that affected you.
Choose a passage
That affected you
And say why it caught you,
Choose words you
Find fascinating.
If a character grabs you
Write about that.
You know how letters
Begin, "Dear Alison" and
Go on from there.

This is new to me,
And it will be new to you.
You won't choose
Books well, some will
Be too easy, some too hard.
There will be adjustments,
But we are going
To be relaxed
About doing this.

Ms. Burns

Reading and writing
Belong together,
And eventually
They are meant
To be shared.

Ms. Burns

Pressure and Challenge

I live in a pressure-cooker,
There's my husband's job
He brings tension home
About his sales.
Paul brings tension home;
I bring it too.
And someone usually
Isn't feeling good.

I never feel caught up;
Look at that stack
Of papers on my desk
I'm always behind
In reading and writing.
I guess that's pressure.

When I began to teach
Ten years ago
I don't remember the pressure.
Today it is different:
Kids with disabilities,
Emotional and physical
And all kinds of legal problems.
When Marshall blows,
Or I see marks
On Amadeo's face,
Or Stacy's fear or anger
I can feel it in my stomach.

But then come the tests
Local, state, and federal.
On top of all these kids
Trying to grow.
Then there's the test preps.
That's new from when I began.
I challenge them every day
Press them hard
To do their best,
But the scores never match

@ Ms. Burns

Their real change.
They tell the child
You are behind.
Amadeo paints,
Does poorly in writing.
Stacy struggles in reading
But is a whiz at math.
All this tells me is
I'm behind as well.

Do you have any extra
Rolaids handy?

4

Reflections for Discussion

Marshall: Explosions, Dogs, and Baseball

You are moving closer to Marshall now. You will be discussing his makeup with colleagues and also with children. I have indicated what to discuss with one or two friends as well as what to talk about with children. I find that children are just as interested in the makeup of Marshall as I am. You will find that children can handle these questions, especially when you say, "I find that some of these questions are quite challenging. See what you can do with them." You are entering the worlds of the home and of school.

You have just finished listening to or reading poems about Marshall. First, what do you make of him? At the least he is very complex. His parents are not around to raise him. Thus, he must have suffered wounds that have become part of his emotional history. We have to remain neutral about his history; it is simply unknown to us. Granny steps forward, saying, "Somebody's got to do it." His grandmother has difficulty with him, yet she is very skilled at raising children.

As volatile as Marshall is, there are some positive elements that characterize his makeup. Consider some of his out-of-school elements that may reveal more about him.

For Teachers

1. Marshall is a living time bomb. Do you have any children in your classroom who are volcanic, ready to blow with the slightest provocation? If you have any children like Marshall, how do they affect the room's atmosphere?

2. Put yourself in Granny's shoes. If you were to speak, what would you say? Talk about Marshall and your own situation in trying to raise your grandson.

3. Like many children, Marshall sees a word he doesn't know and lapses into self-recrimination. What would you recommend to Ms. Burns to help her with Marshall's reading problem?

4. How does Marshall's size impact the classroom? Look at the two or three largest boys or girls in your room. What is their impact?

5. Marshall has one interpretation of Ms. Burns asking him to focus. What would Ms. Burns' interpretation be of using the word *focus*?

6. There is a day when Ms. Burns just "loses it." Talk about the days when you've felt like Ms. Burns.

For Teachers and Children

1. Find which children have pets in your classroom. Please consider the range of pets, from iguanas to Saint Bernards.

2. Pets may be the most humanizing element in your classroom. They can turn the most aggressive student into at least a caring person. Some children don't have pets yet they wish they did. For those who don't have them, let them draw or write about pets they might like to take home.

3. Does Marshall have a soft, more tender side, even a sense of humor? If you have students like Marshall, what do you look for that you might emphasize?

4. Marshall believes that writing is easier than reading. Discuss and comment on his reasons.

5. You may have questions and invitations of your own for both colleagues and your children.

6. Do you think it would be possible to have parents attend such a workshop? You would expand the invitation in number 5.

Gina: Horses, Ballet, and Reading

Gina is the tallest young woman in the class. She says, "Marshall doesn't mess with me." Gina has an awareness about herself that is unusual. "I tell secrets to myself. I am a show-off." She is highly articulate when writing chapter books and reads aloud to the class if Ms. Burns asks her to read.

For Teachers

Discuss the taller girls in your room. Discuss the shorter girls in your room. What is different about them? What are the advantages and disadvantages of being tall . . . or short? Which children seem to be unaware of being short or tall?

For Teachers and Children

Do you think that Gina is unusual in how she reflects on events, such as adults kissing on the terrace or her delight when Lanore pulled a muscle?

Do you think that Gina is manipulating her mother through her tears, or is she genuinely sad about her situation?

For Young Women

1. Do you think it is unusual for young women to be conscious of horses? Do women read about horses in your room? Or maybe boys do as well.

2. Gina is very conscious of being a public school person. What does she take in that brings this to consciousness?

3. Ponder this notion: Gina is very competitive.

4. Consider the way Ms. Burns handles the disagreement between Marco and Gina.

5. What unanswered questions do you have about Gina? What are you wondering about?

6. Discuss the dilemma that exists between Gina and Amadeo. How does each of them handle the problem? Amadeo loves Gina, but does Gina love him?

Marco: The Yankees, History, and Immigration

Marco is the son of a dentist. Marco gets As in school, and instead of praising him, his father says, "Well, that's what you are supposed to get."

Marco comes from a large extended family with one wing that cheers for the Mets while his family roots for the Yankees. When the sauce is cooking, he knows that the Yanks will play the Mets. There is much rivalry between the families but it is all in good fun.

His younger sister, Dorothy, wants to do what he does, like go to a Yankee's baseball game. Marco almost feels sorry for her. But when she takes his CD he wants to punch her.

Marco has a best friend, Andy. They play baseball together and they also read history books. They are even writing a story about the South.

For Teachers

1. Marco and Andy are best friends. Some children have many friends and others not as many. Consider the relationship between study and friendship. Do children challenge each other, or do they just pursue studies alone?

2. Discuss the effect on Marco when Ms. Burns could name every player on the New York Yankees. How did each regard the other after this disclosure?

3. Are there some specific cultural, factual details that you need to consider in order to bring the classroom together for learning?

4. Are there some nouns you would add to Marco's profile? Consider choosing three verbs that would best describe Marco.

For Teachers and Children

1. Consider the dilemma presented to both Dorothy and Marco. Is there a better way to handle the situation? There are only two tickets for the game and Marco sits right behind the dugout.

2. Gina and Marco are at loggerheads over what to do with their immigration unit. Marco brings artifacts to their discussions about immigration and Gina doesn't have much to bring yet tries to force the direction of their research. Look at the immigration unit through the eyes of Marco, Gina, and Amadeo. Ms. Burns asks them to solve their problem. Can they? Will they?

3. Look at the problem of Marco going to the doctor from Marco's point of view and then his mother's point of view.

Stacy: Cooking, Mathematics, and Ethnicity

Stacy is a young girl who enjoys applying mathematics to her cooking. She cooks and then eats what she cooks, which means that she is a bit overweight. Her mother heaps praise on Stacy: "With you in the house I never have to go to the bakery." In contrast with Imelda, Stacy is very conscious of her appearance. Imelda is slim and fashionable; Stacy does not like her appearance. The other children in Ms. Burns' room tease her to make her cry.

But Stacy rejects her Puerto Rican heritage. When her father left, her mother adopted her name from home, Robinson. Stacy would like to change her name as well, but her mother cannot afford the cost.

Ponder three verbs that best describe Stacy.

For Teachers

1. Discuss the issue of mixed parentage and ethnic backgrounds. Sometimes it can add to the person's background if accepted, or detract if rejected. Is there a way to find this out? In Stacy's case, Ms. Burns found out by accident.

2. How do you feel Ms. Burns handled Stacy's ethnic problem?

3. Stacy has a reading problem. At least, Stacy perceives it as a problem. Is there more that Ms. Burns could do?

4. Stacy dislikes sharing her work. Is there a way for her to have a better audience situation?

5. Everyone needs to be able to help someone else. Stacy helps Rosalie learn to cook. Who are the children in your room who need to help others?

6. How can Ms. Burns help Stacy and other children get through the reading tests?

For Teachers and Children

1. Stacy is carrying the burden of violence against her sister. How do you think the situation ought to be handled? Discuss the roles of mother, Imelda, and Stacy.

2. Is there a way for Stacy to deal with the students who tease her?

3. Stacy says, "I don't have anything to say." Do you have children in your classroom who mimic the same words?

4. Is there a way for you to learn what Imelda said to Stacy about their father?

5. Rebekah helps Stacy. There are children in your classroom who know how to help. Who are they?

Amadeo: Paints, Pets, and Gina

Amadeo is the smallest boy in the class. Marshall and others pick on him. But Ms. Burns perceives a moment to bring Marshall and Amadeo together through an incident involving a sick dog. Amadeo is ever on the lookout for other boys or girls who might abuse him.

Amadeo's older brother, Angelo, tears up his artwork and gives him regular beatings when Amadeo gets home. Amadeo speaks with his mother, who throws up her hands. She speaks to Angelo but Angelo has so much pain himself that she can't help Angelo. She works two jobs.

At one time the family had a dog named Lightning. But Lightning was killed and the apartment they live in now doesn't allow pets. Amadeo has always wished for another dog. Strangely, Marshall wants Amadeo to come to his apartment to visit with his dog, Sullivan.

Amadeo is a boy alone. He sketches, even paints—alone. In his immigration unit Gina notices his clever work and says, "We can use this."

After that Amadeo can't keep his eyes off Gina. Amadeo quietly goes about his artwork until Ms. Burns notices the quality of his work.

For Teachers

1. Ms. Burns notices Amadeo's bruises. She doesn't quite know what to do. Yes, she can report the abuse, but will it lead to more abuse? Discuss the situation.

2. What might Ms. Burns do to further Amadeo's interest in art?

3. How many of your children don't like to go home or be at home on weekends? How can you lessen the trauma for some?

4. Who are the children in your class who need more alone time to create? How can you adjust the environment for them?

5. Will Ms. Burns let Amadeo's mother know about his award? Discuss.

6. Ms. Burns is rightfully proud of Amadeo. Discuss her connection with him.

For Teachers and Children

1. Do you think that Amadeo's friendship with Marshall will last? Discuss.

2. How many children in your room have fallen in love? Try to notice. Will Amadeo's love endure? Will Gina return his love? Speculate. What part does love play in learning?

3. Angelo is beating Amadeo. Speculate on why he is doing that.

4. Should awards be given for art, sports, science projects, and so on? Discuss the culture of awards.

5. Do you think that Amadeo's mother knows anything about his award?

6. Amadeo doesn't feel like an author, especially in writing. How can Amadeo's sense as an author be built?

Rebekah: Violin, Reading, and Family

Rebekah comes from a Jewish family where her brother is working hard to pass his Bar Mitzvah. Both her father and her mother work in several delicatessens, which they own. Her parents are second-generation Jews from Russia.

Rebekah enrolled in a Suzuki violin class as a young child and now she is ten and playing very well. Her best friend, Masha, enrolled with her and they sometimes play together in the afternoon. Rebekah is best friend to Masha and also to many of the children in Ms. Burns' class. Rebekah senses when there is disequilibrium in the class and seeks to restore emotional order, especially when Marshall blows up.

She is a big reader and digests books with abandon, especially the J. K. Rowling books. Writing is more demanding, especially when she switched from writing fiction to crafting a personal memoir about her family.

For Teachers
1. Do you have children like Rebekah who work on the emotional climate of the room without being aware of what they are doing?

2. What are the emotional elements that make up Rebekah's family? Discuss.

3. Discuss the present and future relationship Rebekah has with Masha.

4. Discuss Ms. Burns' approach to helping Rebekah with her transition from fiction to nonfiction.

For Teachers and Children
1. Discuss Rebekah's background in relation to Marshall's blowup. How did Rebekah approach Marshall?

2. Rebekah seems to anticipate Stacy's need. How does she go about noticing Stacy?

3. How does Ms. Burns challenge Rebekah?

4. Is there a way for Ms. Burns or Rebekah's mother to sense what is bothering Rebekah about the planes crashing into the Twin Towers? How can teachers ever learn such matters?

5. Discuss the role of storytelling within Rebekah's family.

Ms. Burns: Paul, Baseball, and Reading

Ms. Burns teaches fifth grade on the East Side of Manhattan. She has been teaching for about ten years. She has recently introduced a unit on immigration as well as a new approach to teaching reading.

She has been married to her husband, Mark, for about twelve years. Her husband wishes she would leave her classroom and not bring work home with her. The work consists of planning and especially the emotional baggage of her problem children. She worries about Paul being alone in the afternoon. If he is ill, she and her husband sit down to talk about coverage for him.

Marshall is her greatest worry. She can't always anticipate his explosions. Most of them center in reading but also when other children invade his turf. It takes about an hour for the class to get settled after one of his outbursts.

Ms. Burns is a Yankees fan through and through. She stunned Marco when she cited the entire Yankees lineup, including the bull pen and coaching staff.

For Teachers

1. Discuss Ms. Burns' balancing act between marriage, son, and school. Everyone's situation is different, yet the matter should be discussed.

2. Name three children you "take home with you." You may want to write your concerns about each or even put your concerns about each into a poem.

3. Discuss the testing of children. What do tests include and what do they exclude?

4. How does your room environment accommodate for a wide range of child interest and ability?

5. Discuss which is better: an organized home, an organized school, or both, or all disorganized. I hope you'll have some good laughter with this one.

6. Discuss the range of all-class activities, for example, singing, choral speaking, and reading aloud.

7. Discuss how you negotiate your teaching with other teachers. Above all discuss your negotiations with your principal.

8. When you discuss point of view and help children recognize that two or more points of view exist, do you feel it slows the curriculum down, or does it build a solid foundation for understanding text?

5

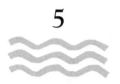

Listening

*M*atthew approached me in class. This was my second year of teaching and I could tell he was wondering which Mr. Graves he'd have to deal with. "You see, Mr. Graves, if I could have slid around the catcher at home plate, I wouldn't be standing here talking to you. Instead, we'd have won, so now I have a different story to tell." Matthew was taking in my whole face and posture. Sometimes Matthew knew I got distracted and looked away. But that day was different. He had all of me, my face, my tongue, my whole self.

Children know that we are often distracted, even rushed. They forgive us. But if I have a steady diet of distraction or I just plain don't listen, then children stop speaking with me. Worse, they stay confined to their desks or talk to others outside, on the bus, or at recess.

How well I recall Mary Ellen Giacobbe at a Harrisburg demonstration! She taught me the value of persistent listening. Here's the scene:

Eighty teachers surround Mary Ellen, who is going to demonstrate the teaching of writing with a dozen fourth graders. "Good morning, children," beams Mary Ellen. "I'm sure you have read many interesting books. Tell me about some of them." She leans toward the children in expectation. But after a good minute and a half, their faces are as blank as when she entered. No one responds.

She makes another request. "You must have been writing about many topics. Tell me about some of those topics." Again she leans forward, her face full of expectation. Again no one responds. I shift in my seat. The audience of teachers rustles nervously; why aren't the children responding?

But Mary Ellen displays no outward tension and continues to smile and wait. Finally, one boy, Ralph, raises his hand. "Yes, Ralph," she says.

"I love my father."

"That's wonderful, Ralph. Can you tell me about it?"

"My Dad was in an accident. A truck hit his car."

Ralph has broken the ice. Other children begin talking about things that have happened to them. A Korean girl tells about not knowing English so she can't tell the bus driver where she lives. Soon all the children are talking, writing, and sharing.

Our hang time may be less than fifteen seconds. Mary Ellen could wait because she knew the meaning of the silence. Just wait and soon someone will speak.

Listening at Central Elementary

A few years ago a number of us noticed that listening was in fourth place on the language arts continuum. Reading was followed by writing and then speaking. Listening was in last place. When Cindy Marten and Staci Monreal walked the corridors of Central Elementary School in inner-city San Diego, hardly a sound was heard. The classrooms were silent. Central Elementary exists in one of the highest crime areas in San Diego. The school enrollment is 1,005 children; for 900 of them, English is not their first language. This was a school placed under corrective action by the state for not reaching state assessment targets. It had two years to improve scores or it would be taken over by the state. The staff's approach to work out of this situation was completely unconventional. They didn't bow to the state mandates. "Why is no one speaking?" they asked. "We have 90 percent English language learners. We can learn language only by using language. If our children are sitting silently all day, how will they ever learn English? The state accountability system demands that they learn enough English to pass an English-only test by the end of second grade."

They realized that maybe the prized quiet school that most educators seek silences the very voices that need to be heard. They soon realized that the conditions could be created to allow the voices to emerge. These conditions centered on listening. If we listen, they knew, the children will talk. Language will develop, voices will emerge. They studied the process of listening and invited the children to begin to talk. Their ears, their hearts, their minds, their bodies all showed that they wanted to listen closely to the children. Once listening—real, authentic listening—was made a priority, the children began to talk and have not stopped talking. The classrooms were no longer silent. They knew the solutions to the failing status could be found by listening to children and employing smart teaching. The children who were meeting state targets were the children who were talking. They all needed to talk. So partnerships were formed. Video footage captured the talkers. Nontalkers started talking.

Listening

The professionals at Central Elementary were actively applying a concept they had learned called *positive deviance*. Seems that Jerry Sternin had written an article about nutrition in Vietnam. He focused on a small group of children who were gaining weight and had decent nutrition in a very poor area. What were they eating? They were eating small shrimp and crustaceans on their rice along with green leafy vegetables. These children were the positive deviants. They were not like the rest of the malnourished children. The solution lay in Vietnam itself; no food needed to be imported. The staff at Central Elementary applied Jerry's article to the children at the school. They looked for children who were thriving and reaching state targets. They found the children who were making it despite coming to school with poor backgrounds. These were the positive deviants. These children were talking and listening to each other. The staff strategically paired the children, got good video footage on what they were doing, and analyzed the DVD during weekly professional development sessions.

That was three years ago. When the children took their reading test after one year of active listening, the school moved out of corrective action status in just one instead of the expected two years. This is an oversimplified explanation of what happened. Strong staff work with many workshops stressed a program of speaking and listening that was good enough to impact the overall academic achievement of this population that had been deemed failing.

Today Central Elementary is forging ahead. They now speak of the Central Elementary way. They speak of their dicta: "Work hard; be kind; no excuses." No excuses was just added in December 2005. These three dicta apply to everyone in the school: administrators, teachers, and children.

In the first year the parents were pleased the school moved out of corrective action so quickly. The staff learned to listen to the children and their voices emerged; they also listened to the parents and their voices also started to emerge. The mission at Central Elementary was being realized.

Remember, this all began with the silence in the building, then exploring positive deviance to find out who the pacesetters were.

Focus on Language

A number of years ago I walked the corridors of Oyster River Middle School in Durham, New Hampshire. Linda Rief had quotations and artwork actually painted on the school walls. Dates of their authorship accompanied the statements. Year after year students would bring their parents to view the precision and beauty of their language.

Be on the lookout for unique ways of saying things. Keep an easel ready for copying down an apt, oral quote. Or examine the pages of students' written language. Children may wish to nominate themselves or someone else may do so. Most classes have two boards, one for oral statements and another for written statements. You might wish to develop criteria for each board. As the year advances, the criteria should rise in quality.

Be on the Lookout

Think back to Chapter 1, when you worked hard to memorize the names of the children in your classroom. You are ever on the lookout to confirm the stories or shards of stories about the children. You may be standing at your door, in the lunchroom, or waiting for the buses to leave. No matter; you are listening for a phrase or sentence that will trigger a question or be revealing of a larger story. Here are some examples:

- I hate salad.
- My dog had puppies yesterday.
- Billy beat me up.
- I can beat up Sam.
- I'm reading *Harris and Me*.
- Who's your favorite author?
- My mom is sick today.
- I hate to ride on the bus.
- I love pizza.
- I'm a whiz at math.

Children are creating stories all day long. Simple statements reveal still larger stories. File them away next to the names you've learned.

Long Thinking

As much as we'd like quick reads and quick writes to dominate our assessment profiles, we get by on the cheap with quick reading. "Fill in the bubble with a number two pencil." How easily the scores come back to us in elaborate printouts.

What we don't know is whether our children can pursue longer-term thinking. In fact, one recent report shows that children who can entertain a question or special interest for sustained periods of time may have an advantage over students who can handle only short-burst thinking. Of course, long thinking requires a very different kind of assessment. This can be assessed only by the classroom teacher or another board of teachers. Research shows that the ability to regulate choice may be a better indicator of intelligence than an IQ score.

Back in the '80s I was interviewing a chief school officer in Aberdeen, Scotland. He said, "Let me tell you how we do it. About the age of nine or ten, our children can elect to pursue special interests with a tutor.

"This means the children get a reading list and ultimately an interview about their reading as well as an examination in a written paper. Some of our children are spending as much as a third to a half amount of [their school] time pursuing their projects and special interests. And that's a lot of listening and speaking as well as reading and writing."

Notice that the children can elect to enter into independent study or be chosen for special study. Both Tom Romano and Camille Allen, as well as other teachers, provide multigenre studies for their college students. In turn, the college students work with children in the schools on their own multi-genre studies. When asked by Roger Mudd on the History Channel, "And how do you get your students at Cornell to love history?" David McCullough replied, "I pass out artifacts and ask them to pursue the origin of the items. When my students learn to discover history, they will learn to love it." Multigenre study is a first cousin to McCullough's statement. The energy is high when discovering information.

When personnel officers are interviewed about desirable characteristics in their candidates, one of the first to be mentioned is, " [He or She] Can design a question and pursue it to the end as well as provide an evaluation on whether they have answered the question or not."

Ms. Burns wants to develop the long thinking of her children and she chose a unit on Ellis Island. There would be good pursuit of family origins on the computers at Ellis Island. Quite naturally there would be growing pains in the groups. Some children would try to dominate and others would be unhappy with their group. (Note the chart on social learning.)

Ms. Burns put children into ethnic homogeneous groups to find out backgrounds to their arrival in the United States. Two groups had difficulty with the assignment. Stacy, although she had a Puerto Rican last name, was at odds with her group. She wanted her mother's name, Robinson. Gina would not let Marco dominate their group process. But when Ms. Burns asked Marco and Gina to state each other's point of view, Marco could do it and Gina couldn't.

Ms. Burns cannot know all of the special interests of her children. She does know about Marshall's love for dogs. She may not know about Gina's love of horses or ballet. Stacy has a special interest in cooking and Rebekah has brought her into her delicatessens to watch the people work. When Ms. Burns spoke about every Yankee in the lineup to Marco, only then did

Marco know of her love for the game, the Yankees, and the players. Give information and soon the facts come back to you from the children. Ms. Burns does know about Amadeo's artwork, but does she know the awful details of his beatings?

Are Your Children Engaged in Both Quick and Long Thinking?

Who are the pacesetters in your room? Naturally I begin with listening because if the child is to have an effect on other children, then listening and point of view have to be at the fore. I move into groups and listen in on their conversations around a certain task, as in planning an immigration study. As Ms. Burns did in her class, I ask, "And what did she just say?" I am confident that if I asked Rebekah what others have said, she would be able to tell me.

Speaking follows listening. How articulate are the pacesetters? Does their language invite comments from others? When they share their writing, what is their response to the group?

Reading follows writing. When they share their books and writing, do they field questions amicably?

Choose one of your children who may be a pacesetter and write about him or her.

First I go for the nouns. Think back to your notes about the children in your middle column. Which nouns dominate, as in *horses, ballet,* and *reading* for Gina? Which verbs dominate, as in *ride, pose,* and *read aloud?*

Gina does pursue her interests. Marshall may not, as reading is a barrier to him. Still, baseball, Yankees, and dogs may be nouns to pursue.

Final Reflection

You have been on quite a journey in learning about the children in your classroom. You began with learning their names by heart and in alphabetical order, if you could meet that challenge. You then began to actively seek noun and verb details to go with each one. Some children emerged quickly (the good students and difficult students).

You helped children negotiate differences and then you moved away from the differences to sing, speak chorally, and work on projects in your neighborhood. All the while they were at work, you were taking notes on children who could sustain thought for longer periods of time. You wondered how to build a community of learners.

Next, you read the poems or you listened to the oral reading of the poems or children may have opted to listen to them individually with headphones.

Ultimately, you moved into both professional discussions and all-class discussions with the children.

Then you moved into listening as an art form and even considered the remarkable work at Central Elementary in San Diego where they were able to put listening at the center and make the gains needed to remove the state monitoring status. These were excellent gains in a very difficult neighborhood. Listening and speaking followed by writing and reading is the best way to advance scores in a balanced framework. Now it is time for you to tell others about your process of learning about your children because when children know you are interested in them, you can expect higher standards in writing.

References

Atwell, Nancie. 1987. *In the Middle: Writing, Reading, and Learning with Adolescents.* Portsmouth, NH: Heinemann.

———. 2005. *Naming the World: A Year of Poems and Lessons.* Portsmouth, NH: FirstHand.

Gladwell, Malcolm. 2005. *Blink: The Power of Thinking Without Thinking.* New York: Little Brown.

Graves, Donald H. 1983. *Writing: Teachers and Children at Work.* Portsmouth, NH: Heinemann.

———. 1992. *Explore Poetry.* Portsmouth, NH: Heinemann.

———. 1995. "A Tour of the Segovia School in theYear 2005." *Language Arts* (January): 12–18.

———. 2004. *Teaching Day by Day: 180 Stories to Help You Along the Way.* Portsmouth, NH: Heinemann.

Graves, Donald H., and Penny A. Kittle. 2005. *Inside Writing: How to Teach the Details of Craft.* Portsmouth, NH: Heinemann.

Kittle, Penny. 2003. *Public Teaching: One Kid at a Time.* Portsmouth, NH: Heinemann.

Mariani, Paul. 1990. *William Carlos Williams: A New World Naked.* New York: McGraw-Hill.

McCullough, David. 1999. "The Art of Biography II." *The Paris Review.* New York, NY.

Sparks, Dennis. 2004. "From hunger aid to school reform: An interview with Jerry Sternin: Positive Deviance Approach seeks solutions that already exist." *Journal of Staff Development,* Winter (Vol 25, No. 1).

Williams, William Carlos. 1946. *Paterson.* New York, NY: New Directions.